Colorful
World of Roses

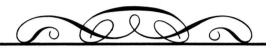

Colorful World of Roses

Xenia Field

PAUL HAMLYN
LONDON·NEW YORK·SYDNEY·TORONTO

FRONTISPIECE:
The floribunda variety Dearest

Published by
THE HAMLYN PUBLISHING GROUP LTD.,
LONDON · NEW YORK · SYDNEY · TORONTO
Hamlyn House, Feltham, Middlesex, England
© Xenia Field 1969
Printed in Italy by Arnoldo Mondadori, Verona
Photoset in the U.K. by Filmtype Services

Contents

This is the first time I have written at any length about the rose. Maybe subconsciously I have put it off in order to get to know the plant as intimately as possible. Living close to Regent's Park, Queen Mary's Garden has been my gorgeous University and Miller Gault, its Superintendent, my kind professor.

But now the time has come to write the book, I am a little awed by the task of describing the subtlety and charm of the old-fashioned roses, the Gallicas, Damasks, Bourbons, Noisettes and other romantic beauties. It will be easier to describe the roses of the last few decades given to us by the modern rosarians. Words can perhaps be found to portray the hard brilliance of Super Star and lavishness of Peace, but to convey the feeling of the rich ivory texture of nineteenth-century Boule de Neige is beyond even the poets.

Again, to write about the flower that has been an emblem of England since the time of the Wars of the Roses is a humbling responsibility. My hope is that my devotion to the rose is strong enough to see me safely through the pages.

XENIA FIELD

Part One

The Soil

The belief that clay soil is the only satisfactory diet for roses is a fallacy. Broken-up clay certainly provides some of the best roses, but a determined gardener on ordinary or light soil, willing to work in a generous amount of farmyard manure, often grows some of the finest blooms.

Success depends on the fertility of the 7 to 12 inches of the top soil, known as the top spit. Its texture can be improved by adding humus which will encourage earthworms and bacteria in their millions to get busy. They can be relied upon to work the organic matter and make it available to plant roots.

As nourishment can only be assimilated in the form of solution, adequate moisture is essential, otherwise the roses will suffer starvation.

Soil Improvement

Humus forming material breaks down the heavy clay (often disastrously wet in winter and baked hard in summer), sets off any alkalinity (excess of lime) and enables the over-light soil to retain moisture. It also darkens the soil which results in making it warmer.

Unfortunately, farmyard and horse manures are by no means easy to come by in town and suburban areas, and home-made compost, leaf-mould or spent hops may have to take its place.

Compost heaps vary from garden to garden, but provided they are of vegetable matter and kitchen waste carefully sandwiched, with the sides and top protected from the weather and kept at a steady heat, then, with the addition of a balanced fertiliser, they should fulfil the roses' needs.

Experts differ as to how long the compost should be kept before digging it into the soil, but it is wise to wait until the contents of the heap are a rich brown and the ingredients so decayed that they are one colour throughout and no longer distinguishable.

Few compost heaps are large enough to supply the amount of food required and the gardener may have to resort to the use of sedge peats, sprinkled with bonemeal or hoof and horn or hop manure.

Perhaps I should add a warning about mushroom manure, of which there seems to be plenty going begging. Rosarian experts as a whole are not enthusiastic about it and consider there is a danger that its heavy lime content may result in chlorosis of the foliage.

The gardener should beware of using lime unless he has good reason to believe the soil is over-acid, such as the failure of yellow and white varieties where the pink and red succeed. In any case, the safe course is to test the soil before taking action, remembering that the rose has no objection to the slightly acid soil in the region of pH 6·5. Not only do some of the big fertiliser and insecticide firms test soil free of charge, but the county horticultural adviser, who can be contacted through the offices of your local authority, is usually willing to give his opinion on soil conditions.

No trouble should be spared in getting the soil right before planting. It is far more time-consuming to improve its texture after the roses are in place, and however considerate the aftercare, nothing compensates for a poor start.

At the risk of boring the beginner, let me beg him not to bury his treasure, nor manure much deeper than the top 12 inches where the rose feeds by means of its fibrous roots – and to leave the precious top-spit where it belongs, forming the top layer of the soil. This is the most important rule of all. If a garden is inherited where the soil has been regularly cultivated for generations, the owner is in luck's way.

Rose-Sick Soil

The soil in the rose bed is apt to become rose sick and exhausted after seven or eight years. A generous dressing of manure, lime and bonemeal does not always put the trouble right. Some believe the sickness may be due to the breaking away of root hairs resulting in a poisonous and lethal deposit, while others hold eelworm rather than soil

Roses in the internationally-famous Queen Mary's Garden, Regent's Park, London

deficiencies responsible for such rose casualties.

Whereas healthy old roses may survive rose-sick soil, new ones introduced possessing an inferior root system will fail to survive. When the soil deteriorates, the gardener has the choice of either choosing a new site for a new bed and the grassing over of the old one; green manuring by sowing a mustard crop, rape or annual lupins and vetches and digging it in; or replacing the tired soil with new loam. Making a new bed is usually the most satisfactory way out.

Meanwhile, the well-known bewhiskered Harry Wheatcroft makes light of rose growing and is fond of saying 'a good heart and a bucket of muck is all that is needed.'

Drainage

The sensitive root hairs need air as well as food and this entails providing efficient drainage so that as the water gets away the air seeps in. To test the rate of run-away, a hole some 18 inches or so deep should be dug and filled with water. If the water drains away during the next 12 hours all is well but if it lingers for longer, double digging is called for. Double-digging involves digging one spit deep and then breaking up the bottom of the trench with a fork without bringing the subsoil to the top.

If the subsoil is solid clay, an application of hydrated lime will help to break it down, but the lime must be restricted to the bottom of the trench and be kept away from the top spit. Liming is not altogether suitable for chalk, gravel and light soils.

The slightly raised rose bed will assist drainage but if after rain tell-tale pools of water stay indefinitely, then some form of drainage system must be provided to run into a main drain or soakaway. When there is serious waterlogging, piping and a sump will be necessary and professional labour is best called in if roses are to thrive on such a site.

The Site, Planning & Design

Planning comes before planting and the roses must be given the best possible position in the garden. They should be found an open site away from big trees, hungry, searching roots and dominant and greedy hedges.

Only recently I have been helping a friend to cut back thick and thrusting chestnut roots that make their way into the rose beds. This is a disheartening undertaking that has to be faced annually, otherwise the coarse tree roots would starve the roses of food.

Although roses are adaptable, beds or borders facing south or south-west usually do best for the plants need sun if they are to bloom generously. Bushes in the shade or facing north are often lush in growth but flowerless. Light shade from the mid-day sun is helpful in enabling the flowers to keep their colour and last longer.

The rose depends on air and elbow room and, if weak, thin wood and diseases are to be expected. Sites where the air cannot circulate freely or which are draughty should be avoided for these conditions are an encouragement to mildew, to which the rose is vulnerable.

Shrub roses with cistus and herbaceous plants, in soft colours. Such mixed plantings must be made with particular care to be effective and pleasing over a long period

Improving Old Beds

Replacing roses in an old bed is always a problem. If the roses have been giving an inferior performance, it may well be that the soil is rose-sick, as I have already indicated, and the gardener would be wise to make a new bed and start afresh rather than fill the gaps left by the departed. After a decade the soil is bound to become exhausted of the roses' particular needs. The fact that veteran plants manage to find nourishment undaunted is due to their extensive roots being strong enough to go in search of fresh and more agreeable soil.

An old and tired bed should be given at least two years rest and is best improved by green manuring (see p. 13). This is a useful way of maintaining the humus content of the soil.

In a very small garden where room cannot be spared for such a change over, a large two-spit-deep hole must be made, the soil discarded and fresh soil introduced from another part of the garden where roses have not been grown before or, better still, some fresh rich loam worked in to improve the soil's fertility. To replace a rose casualty with a new rose in the same hole and soil is neither fair to the newcomer nor its owner.

Roses shown off by a well-tended lawn

Providing the Setting

Rose gardens are lovely because roses are lovely. I only wish we could show them off in a prettier setting more worthy of their beauty. That great gardener Gertrude Jekyll, as far back as 1902, pointed out that we should use our beautiful roses more worthily. 'We are growing impatient of the

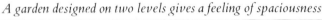

A garden designed on two levels gives a feeling of spaciousness

usual rose garden, generally a sort of target of concentric rings of beds placed upon turf . . . ' she said. And added, 'Beds we have had, and arches and bowers, but very little as yet in the whole range of possible rose garden beauty.'

We are not much better off to-day. The majority of large rose gardens are flat and uninteresting, one much like another, and only made attractive by their enchanting occupants. Most of us are growers and not designers and there are but few such as Vita Sackville-West and Mrs J. Lancaster who can grow and design, and present the informal and dramatic, while making use of contrasting shapes and textures.

On the whole, small gardeners are more adventurous, and I appreciate the suburban gardener who plants his exhibition roses in a straight honest line and no nonsense in the front border; after all, he has little room. But in his back garden he often gives climbing roses freedom to smother his walls and fences with abandonment and festoon, perhaps, a hideous-looking shed.

Gardeners are bedevilled when they come to landscaping. They have been told that a narrow garden is best served by straight lines. To this I add that if the bed is long and narrow, then three or even four rows of staggered bushes should be fitted in. They may have read that an oval bed breaks monotony, that standards will help to cover up any architectural errors. All I can say is that the fewer the beds the better and odd-shaped beds are apt to be tiresome.

Rectangular beds in classical formation with timber pergolas to keep the rose garden secluded from the rest of the garden were a Victorian fashion and are still favoured, but there is no good reason for keeping the roses apart and making them a separate feature. I have to admit the flat, formal rose garden with its stiff bushes gives me little pleasure and I would beg the beginner to seek variation of line and levels.

Pyramidal and globular shrubs, a tall cyprus, yew, holly or juniper and one of the many dumpy, cushiony evergreens carefully placed will make for the right effect. The beginner should visit as many well-designed gardens as he can to derive ideas.

The pink floribunda rose Queen Elizabeth, impressive when grouped, at Royal Lodge, Windsor

Above: *Attractive standard roses, as often seen in the suburbs*

Below: *A bungalow's outline improved by rose plantings*

A Garden on Different Levels

Having deplored the flat, let me suggest a rose garden on two levels. I have complained that the modern landscape architect has given us little new, but I am truly grateful to the designer who inspired the garden on different levels. The sunken garden on two or more levels and the raised bricked-in bed and cut-step terraces are particularly successful in increasing space and make a pleasant breakaway.

I like to see ornaments in the rose garden, sculpture for those who can afford it, and I notice that heads with damaged noses and bodies missing arms and fingers, objects nevertheless, of dramatic charm, are still to be had at a reasonable price. Lead urns, vases and figures are beyond many budgets but there is nothing to prevent the amateur painter turning his attention to a mural or a would-be sculptor providing the statuary.

Home-modelling, however unsuccessful, would be more imaginative and amusing than the familiar-coloured dwarfs, storks and mushrooms which are on offer.

Above: *A raised bed which brings bush roses nearer to eye level is always an attraction*

A successful planting of roses alongside a balustrade

Plants to Grow with Roses

The conventional rosarian shudders at the thought of allowing other plants to share the same bed as his roses. His moral code is strict and his hybrid teas and floribundas merely wave to each other from a distance. But the less rigid who would like their roses to mix with other plants will not find it altogether easy to discover happy associations for their plants. Such friendships are certainly more readily found for the floribunda than the hybrid tea. It is a fact that hybrid tea and floribunda roses do not welcome neighbours with woody roots.

Unfortunately, many herbaceous plants have a shabby look in the late summer and their declining foliage makes them sorry companions. Lilies are, of course, glorious with roses. Those who believe that certain plants are mutually helpful when grown together might like to plant some of the lovely allium or garlic family with their roses.

The story goes that Bulgarian growers interplant onions and garlic with their roses and that they welcome each other's company. Some very exciting alliums with splendid globular heads have been introduced into this country lately from Holland. Fortunately, they give no scent while growing and it is only when they are cut that they offend.

For those who like to give their rose beds a border there are few plants that can compete with the auricula. This little primula has a velvet quality and is most endearing. Pansies and violas, the enchanting little pink, Doris, and of course *Stachys lanata,* the little Lamb's Ear with its silver nap foliage, are all delightful as edgings. But green grass remains the most satisfactory trimming of all.

Below: *Weeping standard roses at their best*

Spring bulbs are not suitable for rose beds as when the time comes for lifting tulips and daffodils, it is almost impossible to avoid disturbance to the roses' surface roots. The large lily bulbs are easier to deal with but the gardener must exercise care when using the fork.

Colour Groupings

When it comes to colour groupings, thought and careful planning are essential, for roses can clash badly, and perhaps those of a similar but different shade clash most of all. I know beds of one colour are not easily arranged in the very small garden, but whenever possible groups should be kept to one colour and orange varieties divorced from red ones.

Fortunately, the old roses and species are less likely to 'growl' at one another than the modern varieties, but gardeners should beware of the brash floribundas.

Right: *An elegantly framed 'dome' of roses*

Below: *Long-flowering floribunda roses that so often compete favourably for attention with bedding plants*

Old brick walls form the most sympathetic background of all for ramblers and other climbing roses

In this delightful garden shrub roses have been given the opportunity to develop naturally and thus form interesting shapes and colour patterns

Left: *Chaplin's Pink Climber, a favourite with many gardeners, bears clusters of large, warm pink flowers*

Below: *Wherever possible, rose beds should be kept to one colour for roses can clash badly. Shown below is the deep pink hybrid tea Ballet*

Planting

The beds should be prepared early in September if the roses are to be planted in the autumn. The second half of October and early November is the best time for transplanting, before the soil has lost its summer warmth and before the arrival of the autumn rains. Northern gardeners would be wise to plant in October.

Failing autumn planting, the gardener content to wait until the end of March may be fortunate enough to miss severe frosts. But, with care, roses can be moved any time during the winter while dormant, so long as the work is not undertaken when the ground is either sodden or deeply frosted.

Planting Distances

When marking out positions for the new roses the bushes should be kept 18 to 24 inches apart. Peace and other strong-growing varieties may be allowed 2½ feet. The standards should be spaced 4 to 6 feet apart.

Spacing between the shrub roses will depend on their vigour but at least 4 to 5 feet should be allowed between each. Climbing roses should be kept 8 feet and ramblers 14 to 15 feet apart. A foot or more must be allowed between the edge of the bed and the first row of roses, otherwise difficulties with the mower are inevitable.

If the roses arrive during a long, hard frost they must be put in a frost-proof building or place until the weather breaks. They will be quite all right left for a week or more if covered with a sack and kept in the nurseryman's packing.

Modern packaging is such that a rose is said to be able to remain wrapped up in polythene for a week or more without harm, but the sooner the plants are opened up and inspected the better. If they are found to be dry they can be damped and re-wrapped until the owner is ready to deal with them.

Should the weather be unkind or the gardener unable to deal with them immediately, the roses should be heeled in under the shelter of a hedge, or in a protected spot. A trench should be dug of suitable length and a foot deep and the plants placed upright, side by side, covering the roots and lower parts of the stems with about 5 inches of soil. They should be firmly trodden in.

Pre-Planting Chores

When planting day arrives, the roses should be inspected. Any leaves left on the plant should be removed to reduce the loss of moisture through transpiration and so avoid shrivelling of the stems. This chore is usually carried out at the nursery.

Roots must be trimmed with the sharpest of secateurs or knife, removing any coarse stump above the union with the scion; broken or damaged root-ends, or maybe a sucker that has escaped the eye of the nurseryman, must also be dismissed. Soft, unripe, autumn-made wood incapable of standing up to winter conditions should be trimmed back, and any tall stems shortened to prevent wind-rock. The gardener must be meticulous in pruning back damaged roots and stems to sound growth.

The planting hole should be of such proportions as to allow the rose's roots to be spread out fully

A rose that has a shrivelled appearance on planting day should be soaked in water and dry roots 'puddled' in a bucket of soil and water; if the 'mud-porridge' sticks to the roots so much the better.

Unhappy looking plants that have been delayed in transit for long periods can be placed in a trench and left completely buried in soil for three or four days. It is surprising how they recover their freshness after such treatment.

The soil in the bottom of the hole must be made friable

The Planting Operation

Now on to the actual planting. First dig out an oblong (rather than a round-shaped) hole, for rose roots usually point in one direction. Beginners told to spread the roots out horizontally 'all the way round' will find the task as impossible as I did when learning. Throw the top foot of soil half on one side of the hole or bed and half on the other, remembering that it has got to go back where it came from after excavation. Now to the veteran's stand-by – any old turf to spare should be chopped up and mixed with the lower spit of soil. It is excellent grub.

A good fortifying planting mixture of medium grade neutral peat and bonemeal sprinkled with hoof and horn should be mixed in a bucket. On heavy soil a coarser sedge peat is advised. Four handfuls of the planting mixture should be placed in each hole and well mixed in with the soil. It is important that at no time should undiluted fertiliser or manure come in contact with tender plant roots.

A small mound should be drawn up in the centre of the hole on which to sit the crown of the plant and the surface should be patted down with the hand to avoid air pockets forming. All should now be ready for planting.

Removing a pre-packed rose from its polythene bag prior to planting

At this stage all soft wood is trimmed back and tall stems shortened

The rose should sit in the hole with its crown on the mound, the roots then being spread out almost horizontally: not all roots grow at right angles and those that do not may be naturally slanted downwards; the gardener should comb the roots with his fingers so that they do not cross one another. Any stubborn root can be kept in place temporarily with a stone or clod of soil. Long roots that are difficult to fit in should be shortened to 12 inches; on no account should they be twisted into place if the hole is too short for them.

The planting mixture can now be dribbled in between the roots and lightly trodden down, later replacing the remainder of the soil (thrown out when planting started) to an inch above the union between the stock and the scion. To ensure that the union of stock and scion is kept to the desired level (never more than $\frac{1}{2}$ inch below soil level) the gardener should tread the outside circumference of the hole first when firming up. The crown will then sit up prettily. There is no such union, of course, on standard roses which are budded on laterals at the top of tall stems, and with these one should look for the soil mark on the stem to gauge the correct depth at which to plant. The roots must be covered by several inches of soil.

Roses must be planted firmly. It has been said that they cannot be trodden in too tightly, but this, of course, is nonsense. Much will depend on the type of soil: if heavy clay is trodden down with a

With the roots spread out carefully, soil is dribbled among them before adding more of the planting mixture

heavy heel it will become compacted and the roots, unable to breathe, will die of suffocation. On the other hand, it is of premier importance that the plant should be securely anchored and the roots brought into close contact with the soil. The gardener needs to go warily to provide all requirements. After planting, he can give the bush a slight shake to test its resistance and stability and firm up once more if necessary.

When spring comes and the gales are over and the soil dried out, the newly-planted should be looked over in case they need a last tread in, the dormant bushes being given particular attention.

The union of stock and scion should not be more than $\frac{1}{2}$ inch below soil level

A final firming is essential to ensure that the plant is securely anchored

Supporting Standard Roses

Standards can be planted in the same way as bushes, with the provisos already referred to, but they must be staked and the support introduced at planting time.

An efficient gardener's tie of eight should be used to avoid chaffing. Iron stakes are ugly and wooden ones usually strong enough for their purpose. The portion to be buried should be treated with a preservative. Labels are very ugly, and more often than not unnecessary. After all, in an ordinary garden there are not so many names to remember.

Climbers and ramblers that call for special support are dealt with later.

Right: *When staking standard roses, position the stake before planting to avoid causing root damage*

Below: *A cross-wrapping of the binding material between stem and stake will avoid chafing*

Below right: *The completed tie*

Pruning

As rose branches grow older they usually lose vigour and vitality and the sap goes into the young shoots, impoverishing the old wood. Every year some of the more mature branches will be seen to have less life in them than the new growth and the flowers they give are likely to be smaller and less perfect. Because of Nature's habit of starving out the older wood, the gardener who wants the best roses must prune.

The most controversial subject among rosarians is when to prune but the majority agree that mid-February in the South to late April in the North is the best time – when the sap begins to rise. But there are gardeners who prune in December or January when the plant is dormant and are confident that this results in early and larger blooms and that the plants will not be more damaged by February frost than those not yet pruned.

The wise gardener will avoid argument and dogmatism. It would seem that the most successful growers favour the spring and later time for pruning.

The pith of a healthy stem is pure ivory-white; any brown marking will denote frost damage. The gardener must cut back to sound wood if the wound is to heal fast and well. And he must not be misled by an apparently healthy eye if the pith above it is discoloured. I can assure him that that bud will never succeed.

Pruning Tools and Their Use

Once again I must impress the beginner with the importance of using the best quality pruners. Cheap or blunt pruners crush the stems leaving an ugly wound that is an invitation to infection and disease, often leading to die-back. He must also beware of forcing or twisting his secateurs.

A short, hooked pruning knife of good quality makes a cleaner cut than the best secateurs and the art of using it can be mastered with a little patience. The cut should slant towards the eye and end just above it, care being taken not to damage the potential shoot. The gardener should hold the shoot at the tip with the left hand and bring it towards him. He should then make the cut by drawing the whole blade across the shoot smoothly and firmly, and, above all, with confidence.

After dealing with canker and diseased wood, the tool employed should be dipped in a disinfectant. A thin-bladed pruning-saw will be required for tough, thick wood.

Leather gloves are essential for this work. My horse-hide gloves have served me well for years.

Cutting out die-back resulting from bad pruning on a previous occasion. Note angle of secateurs and their positioning above side shoot

Pruning Maiden Hybrid Teas

Year-old trees from the nursery require different pruning from established trees. Not only must all weak, spindly stems be cut back to the base but soft wood must also be dismissed. Two or three strong, stark stems of well-ripened wood only should be left, each, it is hoped, with an outward pointing eye about 3 to 4 inches from the union. This severe treatment may give the plant a rather grim appearance but it will build the framework for a strong bush and young shoots will come from low down on the plant.

Should a large number of buds be left on newly-planted trees, the demand will be too heavy on the unestablished roots with too many mouths to feed.

Later on, any dead or unwanted stubs that have been overlooked should be removed; if left, they are likely to become a communal centre for pests.

Root and top growth must balance each other and lush top growth making a heavy demand on the plant's root system should not be allowed during the first year. It is more economical to keep eyes (buds) close to the larder rather than to send food supplies up the long straggling stems to a remotely placed eye.

The Second and Subsequent Years

It is no longer thought necessary to cut back all growth to within 4 or 5 inches of the union. Research has shown that hard pruning does not always present larger blooms than lighter pruning

A hybrid tea rose before pruning

Cutting out dead wood

and certainly it gives fewer of them. The exhibitor with his eye on the show bench may be tempted to prune hard to hold his blooms back, timing them for the July shows.

The gardener should start to prune in the ordinary way by removing all dead wood. He should then endeavour to make an open-shaped bush so that every branch gets plenty of light and air. This entails pruning to an eye that points outwards and removing all twig-like unripe wood or sappy water shoot growth made in late summer that would inevitably be killed by frost. If two branches cross, one must be shortened.

Problems are bound to arise and pruning becomes complex when a weak plant suffering dieback presents the beginner with the ideal bud pointing inwards. It is indeed a temptation to let it stay. On occasion it may be permissible and it is a mistake to be dogmatic, but pruning to an outward pointing bud should be the golden rule.

It is clear that some roses require pruning more severely than others and it will be for the gardener to decide whether the bush needs light, moderate or hard pruning.

Light pruning consists of cutting back to the first or second eye just below the foot-stalks of the flowers pointing in the right direction. It is often a suitable method for plants on light, sandy and hungry soils.

Moderate pruning that suits the average large-flowered hybrid tea, entails cutting back hard all crossing stems and those growing inward while reducing the previous year's main and lateral growth by half to an outward facing eye.

Sometimes two or more growth buds will present themselves in a cluster on the stem. These should be thinned to one bud, rubbing out those not needed with the thumb as soon as they are discovered.

Hard pruning involves cutting the stems back to 4 or 5 inches from the ground to an eye pointing in the desired direction.

Left: All thin wood is removed. Right: The aim is to have an open-centred bush, allowing light and air free access

Exhibitors usually prune hard to three or four eyes from the base which leads to late flowering for the July shows. Not all showmen take the view that this is the best method and there is something in the argument that big bushes give the biggest blooms.

However, it is generally agreed that moderate pruning, allowing the plant to grow 4 to 5 inches taller every year, is sound treatment for garden roses.

Later, as the bush matures and shows signs of loss of vigour and possibly a less furnished appearance, one of the old branches should be cut back annually to within a few inches of the base as a rejuvenating measure. This annual pruning will encourage the required new basal growth and is a golden rule that should be kept.

It will be seen that each bush has its own manner of growth and asks for special treatment but, to look well, a certain uniformity of height has to be kept in a rose bed, particularly if it is of one variety.

Gardeners who inherit neglected roses should, after dismissing the dead wood, cut back to three eyes from the base and mulch the plants generously with farmyard manure.

Flowers for the House

I should like to see owners a little more responsible in the way they pick their roses. One so often sees flowers picked heedlessly with leaves galore but when it comes to putting them in a vase, these are stripped from the stem and thrown into the waste-bin without a thought.

The leaves and the stems are a source of energy, a larder and a life-line to the plant. Faded roses should be broken off at the foot-stalk or cut to a first or second bud.

Picking roses is a form of summer pruning and whenever possible the flower should be cut to an outward facing bud, leaving undisturbed any shoot that is likely to improve the symmetry of the

Left: *Cutting back stronger growths by about half their length.* Right: *Pruning completed*

bush. Long-stemmed blooms for particular vases can, of course, be picked from time to time but with due care and consideration. My warning is to the beginner and over-enthusiastic flower arranger. The constant robbing of foliage and stem inevitably leads to a plant's deterioration, while shortening its span of life.

Pruning Floribundas

The floribunda is undoubtedly the most difficult of the roses to prune. Many a beginner using the knife hard the first year has been disappointed by his plant's performance; there are those who have murdered their bushes.

The plant should be pruned moderately hard in the spring following planting – to within 6 to 9 inches of the ground, cutting back where possible to four or five eyes.

Two forms of pruning will be necessary in the second year. New main shoots from the base of one-year-wood should be pruned lightly; older and weak wood should be pruned to one or two eyes to encourage basal growth.

If the bush is on good soil and is doing well, new shoots will appear from the base. Provided these do not crowd the centre of the bush, they should be lightly pruned and allowed to remain, removing any flower-head to the first healthy eye.

By lightly pruning young and moderately pruning older growth, dismissing old wood and encouraging new, it should be possible to keep the rose flowering continuously through the summer. A floribunda should never carry wood of more than two years standing other than at its base.

With correct pruning, the bushes will remain the same height for 25 years or more. If an increase in height is wished for, then the healthiest growths should be spared the knife for 12 months and lightly pruned the following year. This is the way in which a hedge is built up.

A plant must grow freely if the gardener is to carry out the drill suggested and, for this reason, the soil must be rich and the feeding generous. The open structure of the bush must be maintained. An overcrowded centre of spindley growth makes a happy hunting ground for pests.

A beautifully proportioned rose garden, the component parts of which are in complete harmony

Ramblers and Climbers

The ramblers and climbers possess different, clear-cut characteristics and these should enable the gardener to distinguish one from the other.

The true rambler such as Dorothy Perkins and American Pillar, hybrids of the white *Rosa wichuraiana,* throw up slender, supple and yielding stems from the base every year.

The climber Golden Showers, Climbing Picture and Climbing Shot Silk and others, are less generous with their growth and their unpliable stems are apt to break under strain.

The pruning necessary for the plant will depend on its classification and in most cases is best done with secateurs. If the plant has been well-trained and tied to a support, pruning and the annual overhaul should be an easy matter. The training involves tying in as many branches as possible horizontally, spacing them at least 18 inches apart so that they get light and air.

The climber rather than the rambler depends on this schooling, for, as the gardener is aware, Dorothy Perkins manages quite happily to mount a pillar upright while flowering generously.

Horizontal training not only assists the gardener to cover the wall or support effectively, but controls the free flow of sap which results in encouraging more blooms.

Not long ago I zig-zagged a Climbing Ena Harkness that had not flowered for a number of years round a pillar: I was delighted to see it rich with buds last summer. But in so doing, I had to watch that the brittle stems did not break.

The neglected rambler or climber out of control may be best cut back to within a foot or 18 inches of the ground, even though it means sacrificing next year's flowers.

Pruning Wichuraiana Ramblers

Group 1. This group includes Dorothy Perkins and Crimson Shower. The rambler will come to no harm if left untrimmed for a year or so after planting but it should be tied in. During the second year, after the plant has flowered, all the previous season's growth should be cut down to the ground and new stems trained in. These stems will provide the growth and flowers for the following season and should be left in their entirety, being carefully tied to a support.

Pruning is often simplified by untying the rose, laying it flat on the ground and pruning it there.

Shy performers that have made little new growth may be allowed to retain some of the current year's stems but the laterals should be reduced to two or three eyes. Roses on the older wood are unlikely to be as large or of the same high standard as those rising from the young growth at the base.

Pruning Other Ramblers

Group 2. This includes varieties that throw up only occasional basal stems, the new growth coming from older wood higher up.

Gardeners who have had some experience of these plants will have noticed their tendency to become bare at the base. From time to time an old stem must be cut back to an eye a foot or so from the base in an endeavour to encourage fresh basal growth.

If the tree becomes an eyesore, it is well worth taking it down and letting it lie flat on the ground in the hope that this may induce it to break and form new buds.

Old wood high on the tree should be cut to where a young shoot is ready to take over, the shorter laterals being pruned back to two or three eyes and the tree's leading shoots being given their head.

This group should be pruned as soon as flowering has ended.

Inevitably, old wood becomes unproductive and should be cut out to above the junction of a strong side shoot; the gardener must use his judgment, removing branches in proportion to new growth. Laterals only is the general rule, for lovely roses often appear on elderly canes.

The finger-thick stems should be kept rather than the coarser ones. Side shoots of reasonable length, a foot or so, can be maintained, but should they lengthen to a yard, they must be controlled otherwise they are apt to rob the leader of nourishment. Heavy, demanding top growth is often starved of food and is responsible for the many plant demises.

Climbing Hybrid Tea and Large-flowered Varieties

Group 3. This consists of climbing hybrid tea types and large-flowered varieties, most of which are not as free-flowering as their parents. They are excellent climbers for walls and pergolas; the less exuberant are suitable for a pillar and all members will form a dramatic feature on a green carpet of lawn.

New growths should not be pruned and the knife merely used to keep the rose within bounds, but, of course, old and shabby branches must be dismissed.

Beginners are warned that newly-planted climbers of this category must not be pruned severely during their first year after planting, otherwise they may make it an excuse for reverting to bush form.

Pillar Roses

Group 4. This includes the moderate climbers or pillar roses and all the pruning required is the removal of dead, old or worn out wood, while keeping the plant nicely shaped. Again, the first year pruning should be light or not at all. Should climbers fail to break with fresh growth, syringing with water will sometimes induce them to do so.

Failing this, the plant should be taken down and laid flat on the ground for a few days in the hope that it will reward its owner for his trouble by making fresh shoots.

Training the rambler and climber is a time-consuming business, but I hope I have been able to explain away some of the mystique of pruning. Maybe the gardener will find it easier if he starts tying in at the base, dealing with shoot after shoot and working upwards.

It may take a climber a few years to settle down and three or four years to be at its best, but what more wonderful than a deep red climber on an old brick wall or pillar.

Standards

The standard rose has not the vitality of the bush rose and does not react well to hard pruning every year. Severity with the knife can be dangerous.

Dead and weak wood must be cut out, making room for the strong, healthy shoots. I notice that some rosarians paint any formidable wounds with a waterproofing preparation to protect the wood. Not all varieties are free branching and older wood may be kept on occasion, provided it is healthy.

Floribunda standards often produce strong shoots from where the plant was budded. These shoots should be cut back to four eyes. The floribunda standard can face up to fairly hard pruning and flowers more effectively if cut back to main growth shoots rather than sub-laterals.

Weeping Standards

The weeping standards are in the main budded rambler roses on Rugosa stems that should be pruned in a similar fashion to ramblers. The new growth should be encouraged, and the previous season's wood that has flowered dismissed.

Older wood, if lively with new shoots, even if a little way down the stem, may be left. Laterals should be cut back to within an inch of the main stem.

Wire trainers, umbrella-shaped, may or may not be to the gardener's taste. They certainly show off the rose and any rebellious cane that refuses to conform can be tied down and trained into place. The Wichuraiana hybrids with strong, stiff stems should be mastered early when the growth is young and willing.

Hedges

The majority of varieties benefit by hard pruning to the fourth or fifth eye the first year after transplanting. When established, dead and weak wood must be removed and the roses kept nicely shaped to the desired height. Toughs like the Rugosa types respond to hedging shears in the spring.

I am afraid a number of unsuitable varieties are sold as good hedging plants and the beginner must beware of this. The successful hedgemakers are by nature strong and bushy in habit. Even the variety Queen Elizabeth needs discreet pruning, restricting her outward shoots, otherwise she may get leggy, confining her glorious flowers to the top of the hedge.

Polyantha Pompons

These are the bushy dwarfs that require very light pruning when dormant. However, they should be firmly kept to the same height when planted in beds if they are to be fully effective. Dead wood should be removed and faded flowers cut back to an upper eye.

Miniatures

Budded and grafted plants are apt to lose their miniature habit as they grow up. The knife will not hold them back permanently and, resenting hard pruning, they may say good-bye.

Plants on their own roots should be bought if true miniatures are wanted. Much of the plant's growth will die back in the winter, being in the main flowering growth with little foliage.

Shrubs

This group includes the species, musk, moss roses, those known as old-fashioned and others. The gardener must observe which of these flower on the new wood and which on older wood so that he can prune accordingly. For instance, the majority of the old-fashioned roses flower on two-year-old wood, so at least some of this must be maintained if there is to be blossom the following summer.

Leggy plants have to be rejuvenated in the usual way by cutting out an old wood stem to its base and reducing weak growth to 12 inches from the ground. But the species should be pruned with particular care for fear of spoiling the beauty of their arching stems and delightful way of growth.

The Royal National Rose Society's booklet *Roses – A Selected List of Varieties* will be found a help to beginners who are uncertain to which

Left: *A shrub rose before pruning.* Right: *After pruning with the old wood removed and weak wood cut back*

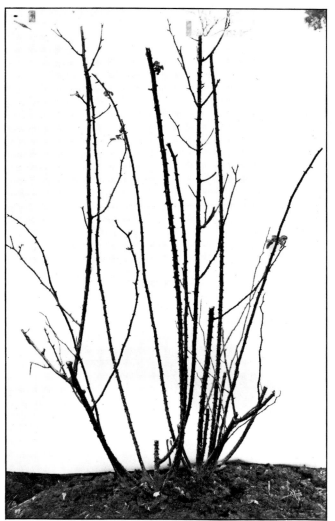

group their roses belong and the treatment they should be given.

My last tip to the gardener regarding pruning is to accustom himself to using the knife by cutting various twigs of no importance in woodland and hedgerow – cutting boldly with a smooth clean, upward slope. When accomplished and confident he should start on roses requiring light pruning only. Once assured and to some extent experienced he can go forward with the hard pruning.

Roses in Pots Under Glass

Roses under glass, usually brought inside in November, should be pruned during December or early January. They should be kept cool – at outside temperature but excluding frost – before and after being cut back.

Plants should be watered very moderately while undergoing the knife and be in no way hurried to break into growth otherwise weak growth and poor blooms will follow.

Hard pruning is advised for the first years, dismissing all weak and crossing wood while reducing the ripe wood to two or three eyes. It is hoped that after the first year sturdy basal growths will appear and be strong enough to replace some of the old wood that can be cut out. If basal growth is lacking, then the old wood must be retained and the laterals shortened to the point of the previous year's pruning cut.

The gardener should aim at a well-shaped and nicely balanced plant – dwarf rather than overgrown, and five or six stems should suffice. It will be noticed that fewer eyes break into growth under glass. However, a bush pruned to 8 or 10 inches in the spring will develop into a strong bush of some 3 feet by the autumn. Such plants should not be fed after July, for late growth that will not ripen is wasted effort.

Lastly, pot plants should not be allowed to overflower and quality rather than numbers should be the aim.

Suckers

Most rose bushes are made up of the top growth of a cultivated variety and the root system of some form of wild rose. The purpose of this undertaking, or budding as it is called, is to provide the cultivated variety with extra vitality from a more vigorous root system than it possesses itself.

There is one inevitable disadvantage to the operation – the wild rootstock sends up growths or suckers from below the union and if these are left to themselves they will, because of their strength, outgrow the more delicate variety.

The only reliable way of identifying a basal growth is by scraping the soil away from the budding point or union and tracing the sucker back to its source. If the growth comes from above the budding point it is of the cultivated variety and should be kept and cared for. If the growth comes from below the union, then it is of the wild rootstock and must be dismissed as soon as sighted.

A sucker should, if possible, be pulled away rather than cut, there being more chance by this method of ensuring the removal of any further eye. But if the sucker is old and unwilling to come away, then the gardener should make a nick cut into the stem or gouge out the unwanted growth with a small trowel. This is wiser than seriously disturbing the rose's roots or taking the risk of pulling the plant up altogether.

On no account should the sucker be cut off at ground level as this has the unfortunate result of encouraging more suckers of greater strength.

It is a fallacy that suckers can be identified as wild growths if they carry more than five leaflets to the leaf. The fact that ramblers have seven leaflets and hybrid teas and floribundas five to seven, makes nonsense of such a test.

Suckers sometimes form on the stems of standards and should be rubbed out as soon as they are spotted.

A COMFORTING THOUGHT

I am glad to be able to say that pruning is easier in practice than on paper. The over-timid with knife in hand must harden their hearts if they are to become rosarians.

A REMINDER

All roses should be examined before the winter and long shoots shortened so that the plant does not suffer wind-rock in the winter gales.

Diseases

There are no shortages of diseases among plants, but only a few are of a really harmful nature to the rose. The most common and disfiguring are mildew, rust and black spot, all brought about by fungi that are reproduced from microscopic spores. Given sympathetic conditions, the spores throw out threads and these explore the surroundings and the possibilities of establishing themselves.

The fungi which attack roses and other decorative plants are all too much in evidence – those that thrive on dead or decaying matter and the parasites that grow on living organisms. But it would seem that the majority are conservative in habit and confine themselves to a species and the enemies of the rose remain faithful to their host.

Fungi spread by the million and, being light and airy, they travel with the breeze leaving their spores on rose after rose as they float along. The gardener may assist them by negligent handling of the affected roses. Once the spore has devoured its own supply of nutriment it must look elsewhere for nourishment and attacks and robs the rose.

The size, shape and colour of the invaders vary and the rose reacts differently to each.

It is regrettable that this chapter on ill-health has to be written but every rose grower must learn to recognise the enemy. He may comfort himself in that if he keeps his plants well fed and cared for they will be less vulnerable to attack than the poorly cultivated.

Good hygiene is worth more than all the advertised sprays, but please avoid unnecessary coddling. Some years the weather is against the gardener. Wet periods leading to lush growth, hot days followed by cold nights, light dew enabling spores to stay are all favourable to disease which, of course, is more prevalent in some areas than others.

My sympathy goes to the gardener with a neighbour who has a collection of miserable disease-ridden rose bushes. The neighbour who lies stripped and stretched out on chair or grass with eyes closed trying to get a South of France tan. Fortunately for his peace of mind, the mildew spores blowing over the hedge are too small for the gardener to see with his naked eye.

Mildew

This is the most common of rose diseases to which many of the older varieties of hybrid teas and ramblers confined to walls, balustrades and draughty positions are particularly vulnerable.

Mildew is always with us, and some years there is a positive epidemic of the disease and many roses dusted with the depressing white flour powder in almost every garden. The first signs of its presence are white-grey spots on the young growth and stems which may become slightly red-purple as the trouble develops. Once present, the attack spreads fast. Foliage is misshapen, buds remain unopened and flowering is brought almost to a halt. Neighbouring plants will soon become infected.

The Wichuraiana hybrids with their glossy leaves often evade attack, although they are not immune, but the soft-leaved hybrid tea seems to have little defence. Lovely and beautifully-scented Crimson Glory seems to invite the disease.

A well-known rosarian described mildew as the rose's common cold and sprayed against it every two weeks from the middle of July until towards the end of August. Otherwise it was, he said, bound to appear on some of his roses. Courtyards and enclosed gardens where the air has difficulty in circulating are favourable to mildew and disease-resistant varieties should be chosen for these areas.

The gardener's natural complaint is that as soon as he has fought off an attack a severe variation in temperature may well start another onslaught straightaway. However, mildew is curable and, disfiguring as it is, is the lesser of the three evils operating on the surface of the rose.

A spray made up of ordinary washing soda diluted at the rate of an ounce to a gallon of water will be strong enough to deal with a mild attack and is useful as a preventive measure.

The fungicide dinocap is an effective control for

A rose leaf affected by mildew

mildew. The importance of adhering strictly to the manufacturer's instructions when using fungicides cannot be over-stressed.

Black Spot

Black spot is not as common a disease as mildew but it is more destructive and can ravage a rose bed in a few days. It is not, however, a killer. The fungus strikes in warm, wet weather when the foliage is almost fully grown. Often starting in the South-west in late June, it is fast to spread and may be seen all over Britain by August. Industrial areas are generally spared, being protected by sulphurous fumes.

Black spot appears in the form of small black specks on the top of the leaves and develops to almost circular black or purple-black spots of $\frac{1}{4}$ inch diameter with fringed edges. On occasions, the spot covers the entire leaf.

As the disease gets hold, shining black dots arrive in concentric circles on the surface of the spot. Each dot may hold a few thousand spores

and these only too easily get wafted on to the surface of a rose leaf where they expand laterally and vertically.

When heavily infected the leaves will fall much earlier than normal and the bush may be stripped before June. The gardener should remove affected leaves and burn them. It must now be expected that the disease will spread to the stems, blistering and discolouring them.

There is no permanent cure for black spot. All

Rose black spot

the gardener can do is to concentrate on growing healthy roses that will resist the enemy and follow a programme of prevention. Few roses (except possibly Wichuraiana varieties) are immune to black spot but some suffer from it more severely than others.

Careful hygiene is essential. Fallen leaves likely to be contaminated with spores must be collected and burnt to prevent further infection. Once seen to be infected, a leaf is better removed than allowed to fall, and diseased stems and twigs must not be left on the ground.

Gardeners in the South are wise to start spraying against the fungus at the end of June while those in the North and Scotland can wait with fair safety until mid-July. If spraying very early in the season, it is wisdom to use the fungicide at half strength on delicate young foliage.

The leaves must be completely covered top and underside and this carried out when the foliage is dry. If there is a covering of fungicide on the leaf before a rain-fall all the better for the spores will not then be washed on to the soil below. As a precaution the ground beneath the bushes should also be treated.

Spraying with colloidal copper emulsion is helpful in killing the spores or at least bringing them to a standstill. Captan (poisonous to fish) has for many years been the specific control for black spot. The new product Phaltan, which controls black spot, is combined with Karathane (dinocap), which controls mildew, in Murphy's Rose Fungicide and seems to be preferred by knowledgeable rosarians. Maneb is another effective spray.

Perhaps I should remind gardeners that captan must not be used with colloidal copper emulsion that controls mildew or rust – though dinocap can be used with captan. Whatever fungicide is chosen, the regularity of the spraying programme is of major importance.

Mulching acts as a trap for falling spores. The mulch must be renewed at the end of the season and dug in well away from the roses, otherwise the fungus would repeat its cycle the following year.

A small purple spotting of the foliage due to a mineral deficiency often leads to unnecessary anxiety. A bucket of manure or a generous application of a reputable general fertiliser is the answer.

Rust

No cultivated rose appears to be immune from rust and the glossy leaves are particularly vulnerable. We are still in the dark as to the incidence of the disease other than it seems to be more prevalent in districts where there are early and heavy dews.

This can be a serious disease and plants severely attacked often die during the first year of the infection. It is variable in behaviour, being prevalent in the West Country while never seen in many gardens in the South. However, almost

Rust, showing the pustules on the underside of the leaf

absent throughout the country for several years, it will often return in a virulent form and ravage the rose beds.

On its first appearance in early spring small sulphur-coloured, pimple-like swellings will be noticed on the undersurface of the leaves. In the next stage, about June, they become bright yellow and when late summer comes they ultimately turn black. The leaf deteriorates, dies and falls.

These pimples or pustules will spread to stems, destroying buds. The onslaught leaves permanent scars and blemishes on the stems that are an invitation to other fungi, including canker.

There is no entirely satisfactory treatment for rust, the difficulty being that it does not vegetate like mildew on the surface of the foliage, but within the tissues of the plant. Fallen leaves must be carefully collected and affected stems cut out and burned. The soil beneath the bushes should be turned over and spores, so far as possible, rendered inactive.

It would be wise to sacrifice and burn a single infected plant in the hope of halting an epidemic. Thiram, zineb and colloidal copper are the controls used against the trouble, these being applied from the end of May onwards, as directed.

Fortunately, the incidence of the disease has diminished since the war.

Chlorosis

Yellowing is often the result of poor drainage or unsatisfactory watering or possibly lack of light, but chlorosis, a physiological disorder, is more marked and serious than this. The loss of green colouring and part or complete yellowing of the leaf beginning with the young foliage tells the tale.

Chlorosis is due to iron deficiency. It is prevalent on chalky land where the excess of lime in the soil decreases the availability of iron. Without chlorophyll the plant cannot manufacture carbohydrates necessary to its growth and well being and soon faces starvation. The disorder usually appears towards the end of spring.

Research is constantly being undertaken to see if there is a method of unlocking the iron in the soil and making it available to the rose but as yet there is no satisfactory answer. Meanwhile, the scientists offer the gardener iron chelates marketed as Sequestrene to correct the deficiency.

This product is soluble in water and can be used as a spray but is best applied to the soil. Sequestrene Plus is helpful in dealing with both iron and manganese deficiencies and must, as always, be used strictly according to the manufacturer's directions. Maxicrop offer a version of their seaweed manure with an iron content as an aid.

Meanwhile, the gardener can play his part in counteracting the disorder by treating the rose bed to generous amounts of organic manure which will do much to improve a chalky subsoil and alkaline condition.

Canker

This trouble usually comes from a wound in the bark giving an insect or fungus a chance of entry. Or, of course, by unhappy pruning with blunt bladed pruners. A browning of bark and long disfiguring cracks in the stem announce the infection. There is no cure for this but the gardener can often save his plant by ruthlessly pruning back discoloured stems to sound wood.

Canker, a trouble which must be ruthlessly eliminated

A REMINDER

The gardener will make his own programme to suit the situation.

MILDEW: Spraying may begin in the middle of July and should be repeated every ten days or fortnight as necessary until the end of August.
BLACK SPOT: Spraying may start at the end of June (or mid-July in the North and Scotland) and go on as required until the end of the season.
RUST: Spray from end of May onwards, as directed.

Spraying is best done in the evening. There is a risk of damage if it is carried out in hot sun or when there is a drying wind.

The trouble about diseases and disorders is that they often establish themselves before they are recognised. The gardener is advised to keep a watchful eye on his roses when he will soon be able to differentiate between those ills that slightly disfigure and those that damage and kill.

Pests

Damage by pests is easy to spot. Laying their eggs where they will, they feed by biting the leaves and fruits of plants or by puncturing leaves and sucking the juices, and they infest the plant.

Aphids (Greenfly)

Is there a garden without them? I doubt it. They arrive on the underside of leaves, young shoots and flower buds, and there is one species that also attacks the roots.

A number remain faithful to the rose throughout the year while others, after a stay, pass on to different plants. The gardener who over-feeds with nitrogen and so causes his roses to make soft growth will never be short of greenfly.

The aphids puncture the leaves with slender stiletto stylets and the plants are ravaged to provide the quantity of nutriment required. Far more sugar is consumed in the process than the aphids can absorb and this is, therefore, passed through their digestive system and excreted. The sticky deposit is known as honeydew and is remarkably attractive to ants, flies and other insects. It is often followed by an unpleasant black mould.

It is fortunate for us that the aphids have their opponents. The birds are a help and so are the ladybirds and their larvae. The hover or serphid fly with wasp-like markings that hovers and darts, and its larvae, are a considerable check on the aphids and we should also be grateful to the lacewing and ichneumon fly for defending the rose.

There are a number of effective insecticides. I favour those safe for the operator such as pyrethrum. They should be applied as a mist spray, giving full coverage without wasteful drenching or drip. A sprayer capable of delivering insecticide with considerable force is essential for this purpose.

Systemic insecticides readily absorbed not only by the plant's foliage but by the roots are, as they develop, likely to be more used in the future than the former contact poisons. Stomach poisons are helpful in protecting foliage against sucking insects and I have found Abol-X, which contains

Greenfly on rose buds

the chemicals gamma-BHC and menazon, particularly effective as an early May and July spray.

Meanwhile, the finger and thumb, always ready for action, remain one of our most valuable stand-bys on such occasions.

Thrips

These are the thunder-flies that buzz and swarm around on a hot, dry summer's day. They disfigure the rose, mottling the foliage and giving it a marbled look, while distorting young growth. Buds are discoloured and malformed and flowers often fail to develop.

The offender is black or dark brown, $\frac{1}{8}$ to $\frac{1}{10}$ inch long with wings and a nasty mouth not unlike that of the aphid. It is capable of sucking and mashing rose tissues and of burrowing its way into the very centre of the bud.

A leaf damaged by rose leaf-hopper

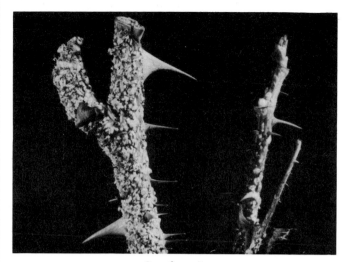

Scurfy scale

The early June hatch is usually more damaging than the later autumn incubation. Insecticides for controlling greenfly and DDT will be found effective.

Scale Insects

Healthy roses are seldom troubled with the incrustations of white-scale insects. They go for the old, tired and unhealthy, and elderly shrub roses. Scurfy scale is more common than the brown or nut kinds and roses on briar stocks often have their stems overlaid with their white, flat scales. This is another insect supplied with sucking apparatus in the form of stylets and a severe infestation will check the rose's growth.

Malathion applied as directed in the spring will control scale insects.

Moths

The moth's larva, the caterpillar, is capable of chewing or skeletonizing a rose leaf with its biting mouth. The Tortrix moth or 'rose maggot' burrows its way into bud and flower. When in fear it can be seen taking flight by letting itself down a silken thread. Often to be found wrapped round in a leaf, a pinch from finger and thumb will settle the matter.

The thrip deposits its eggs in the tissues of the foliage and flowers. Adults manage to overwinter in brick and woodwork and beneath the rose's bark. They are a trouble to the gardener growing roses under glass.

The thunder-fly has a particular liking for lovely hybrid tea Ophelia and her descendants, Madame Butterfly and Lady Sylvia.

This pest can be controlled by spraying with lindane, malathion or derris. The buds must be sprayed at an early stage well before they open.

Rose Leaf-Hopper

This is a yellow-white, active, agile insect, jumping, flying and leaping into the air when danger approaches. It attacks the undersides of the leaves, leaving them pale and mottled during spring and summer. Severe attacks result in leaf fall.

The caterpillars and maggots are more of a nuisance than a menace and can be controlled with pyrethrum.

Cuckoo Spit

The small yellow body is surrounded by a frothy sap and can be dismissed by a forceful spray of malathion, while finger and thumb are handy and cheap.

Chafer Beetles

The flying beetles include the cockchafer or May bug, a large beetle with a black head, the rose chafer, smaller and golden, green wings flecked white, the garden chafer, little more than $\frac{1}{2}$ inch in length and bluish-green, and the summer chafer, a little larger, red-brown and hairy insect.

The chafers begin life as unpleasant grubs feeding and severing rose roots. They lie in a semi-circular position and thrive in sandy soil.

The garden and summer chafers emerge in June and feed when adult on buds and blooms. When arriving in swarms they can cause severe damage. It is important to treat the soil with BHC in order to destroy the grubs.

Sawfly

There are over fifty species of sawflies but the leaf-rolling and slug sawfly are two of the most destructive of them. The leaf-rolling adult – black, shining and not unlike an ant – inserts an egg in the margin of the underside of the rose leaf. The leaflet responds by rolling downwards, protectively covering the egg. When the green-white larva, usually a single specimen, hatches out it feeds on the folded leaf and then attacks other foliage.

The adult sawfly should be sprayed with derris at the flying ant stage. Once the leaf is curled, spraying is of little avail and the leaf should be cut off and burnt, otherwise the leaf-rolling sawfly will build up in numbers and become a menace.

The slug sawfly larva has five summer hatchings that leave a trail of skeletonized leaves behind it. Once appetite is satisfied the insect falls to the ground and forms a cocoon in which it pupates. DDT emulsion gives effective control.

Above: *The distinctive cuckoo spit*

Below: *A leaf damaged by sawfly larvae*

42

Above: *Leaf attacked by leaf-rolling sawfly*

Below: *Damage caused by leaf-cutting bee*

Shot-Hole Borer

Should the shot-hole borer insert its eggs in the stem, the shoot will die and must be cut back to sound wood. Hollow stems that have been attacked in this way through the pruning cut must also be pruned back. A smear of white lead paint over pruning cuts is a helpful protection when the shot-hole borer is active in the neighbourhood.

The Leaf-Cutting Bee

There are a number of species of this bee but *Megachile centuncularis* is the commonest of them. Resembling the honey bee but sturdier in build, the female, with her jaw, cuts out an immaculate smooth-edged circular piece of a leaf or flower petal. This industrious bee is hard to track down, laying her eggs in deep tunnels. However, a spray of DDT will at least discourage her.

Virus

Mercifully the virus rose streak and other forms of disease that have become prevalent in America is virtually unknown in this country. However, every rosarian can play his part in protecting Britain's clean stock by practising meticulous hygiene, sterilizing knives and secateurs and propagating only from healthy stock.

Other Troubles

The jobbing gardener is often described as, and indeed may well be on occasion, a destroyer. He can do a lot of damage to the rose's surface roots with his fork at well over half a guinea an hour. Firm direction by the gardener-owner is the recommended treatment.

Meanwhile, in unfavourable parts of the country the weather does more permanent injury to the rose than all the pests and diseases. A severe May frost will mark and distort young foliage. The small gardener in a very cold area can lightly thatch his bushes or standards with straw or bracken to protect them against the weather.

It must be remembered that the rose has friends as well as enemies, among them the birds, and the likeable ladybird.

Aftercare

After long periods of rose growing, soil is liable to become rose sick. As a result the plants die back and the spindly growth coming from the base of the bushes denotes that the plant's roots are at a standstill. I have described on p. 12 the action that should be taken in such circumstances.

Firming and Staking

When the severe winter frosts are over the roses should be inspected and those loosened by the frost firmed up, but the beginner on heavy clay should beware of compacting the soil.

Plants that have been blown over by the wind may need staking; wooden stakes will last longer if treated with Cuprinol. Where ramblers and climbers require supporting, lasting stakes or posts should be used of sweet chestnut or, if the budget permits, of teak. In wind-swept gardens drain-pipes should be buried in the ground and stakes firmly cemented into them. When using trellis I favour the large-square variety that allows the climber plenty of ventilation and minimizes the disfigurement caused by mildew encouraged by stagnant air conditions.

Weeds

Rose beds are best weeded by hand or carefully pricked over with a fork. The tines must not be allowed to penetrate deeper than an inch for fear of disturbing the rose's roots that feed near the soil's surface. The hoe should be used with the same care as the fork.

Deep tap-rooted weeds are best removed with a small hand fork. The alternative is to use paraquat, a contact weedkiller, which kills plants when it is sprayed on their leaves or stems but which is inactivated on contact with the soil. Naturally, this chemical must not be allowed to touch the roses and this is made easy by attaching a special spray bar to the spout of the watering can being used. Mulching, as described, also suppresses weeds effectively.

Mulching in Spring

A spring mulch of farmyard manure applied in April after pruning and just as the sap is beginning to rise, works wonders, particularly if a dressing of general rose fertiliser, spread at the rate of about 2 oz. to the square yard, is lightly forked in first.

Apply a dressing, preferably organic, of fish meal, meat and bone meal, dried blood, Maxicrop (seaweed manure) or general rose fertiliser. These slow-acting stimulants with a low yield will help the plant over a long period and encourage new growth.

Now comes the task of applying the mulch to conserve moisture, protect roots from extremes of temperature and to keep down the weeds. All rosarians agree that farmyard manure is unbeatable as a mulch, supplying a generous amount of organic material, bacteria and other micro-organisms. The covering should not be more than 2 inches thick and the manure kept away from the stems of the bushes or standards.

Gardeners often complain that the birds scratch the manure over the grass and make the garden look untidy. Sprinkling soil on top of the mulch or netting the dressing down is sometimes advised but is seldom worth the labour involved. On heavy clay soil the manure is best buried so that it penetrates the soil more deeply than if left on the surface. But beware of disturbing the rose's surface roots.

The fortunate country gardener who can pick and choose is advised to apply horse manure on heavy soil and farmyard manure on light soil. For the less fortunate there are a number of alternative mulches.

Garden compost, peat and a balanced fertiliser is an excellent mixture. Peat is a valuable mulch capable of holding the moisture but care must be taken to ensure that it is well soaked before use.

Home-made compost, spent hops and lawn mowings all serve as useful mulches for roses. Lawn mowings are apt to generate heat and the mulch should not be of more than 2 inches thick; it should also be turned over at intervals to prevent it becoming a solid blanket. Mowings should not be used if the lawn has recently been treated with a hormone weedkiller.

A word of warning about sawdust, which is advertised as a good spring mulch; it is said it may lead to nitrogen depletion due to its carbonaceous content, but I cannot speak from experience, never having used it.

May I remind the beginner of the vital importance of applying the mulch when soil is moist after rain or watering, and that fertilisers should not be given during a drought. The British weather usually supplies the necessary rain but should it fail to do so, the gardener can resort to the tap.

At the end of the season the mulch should be removed and dug into the vegetable garden if there is danger of disease spores being present. If the roses are clean and disease free the organic material which is left can be forked into the rose bed at this time.

Fertiliser Applications

If, for some reason, the roses have not been fed and mulched in the early spring they should be given a dressing of complete organic fertiliser in May as they are coming into bud. Apply this at the rate recommended by the manufacturer. For those that have been fed earlier the May feed is an optional treat.

It is necessary to help the roses along during these months after their first flush of bloom. A complete fertiliser will encourage a second performance; it is best given at full strength if organic and at half strength if inorganic.

Soil conditions vary so widely that there can be no unanimity on the right dosage. The grower on chalk will wish to correct the alkalinity while his counterpart on heavy clay may have to supply a dressing of lime every few years.

I can do no better than repeat the Royal National Rose Society's advised application for May and June for those who like to mix their own fertiliser:

Nitrate of potash	..	..	..	by weight 6 parts
Sulphate of ammonia	..	..	..	3 parts
Superphosphate of lime	..	..	..	16 parts
Sulphate of potassium	..	..	..	8 parts
Sulphate of magnesium	..	..	..	2 parts
Sulphate of iron	..	..	..	$\frac{1}{2}$ part

On chalky soils the magnesium and iron should be doubled, and on heavy clay soil if six parts of sulphate of calcium (gypsum) be added it will get the soil into better condition.

These applications should be thoroughly mixed, any lumps crushed down and then scattered over the soil at the rate of 4 ounces (or two small handfuls) to the square yard.

Many gardeners like to make up their own mixture of fertilisers and congratulate themselves that there is a monetary saving. Here is a simple recipe: $\frac{1}{2}$ oz. of nitrate of potash and $\frac{1}{2}$ oz. of sulphate of potash mixed with 3 gallons of water and applied at the rate of 1 gallon to the square yard from the time the buds appear until they open will give surprisingly good results if the treatment is repeated every five days.

Few gardeners have the opportunity of preparing horse or farmyard liquid manure which requires bagging and then soaking in a tub. This liquid should be diluted with water and reduced to the colour of pale straw before being used.

My advice to the beginner is to buy a reputable, well-balanced organic fertiliser ready mixed.

Various Diets

Roses are fairly described as greedy feeders and certainly enjoy a varied diet. Here are a few reliable feeds that will ring the changes:

The well-known Tonk's Rose Fertiliser:

10 parts nitrate of potash
12 parts superphosphate of lime
8 parts sulphate of lime
1 part sulphate of iron
2 parts sulphate of magnesium

This mixture is a great standby, welcome in July. A heaped dessertspoonful should be sprinkled evenly around each bush, care being taken not to let the application fall on the stems of young growth.

Nitro-chalk in granular form can be recommended as a light dressing for over-acid soil and is easily spread on the ground without scorching the foliage. Gypsum is useful for breaking down heavy soil. Dried blood supplies nitrogen and a limited amount of phosphate and potash.

An April dressing of weathered soot will darken and warm the soil, but must be stored under cover for three months in a dry shed before it can be used with safety.

Liquid feeds are usually used by exhibitors as an extra fillip when the plants are in bud.

It is not easy for the beginner to detect the deficiencies in the soil and the requirements of the inactive and unrewarding plant but he can call upon the County Horticultural Adviser for his opinion, and, if necessary, a detailed soil analysis, free of charge.

At the end of August sulphate of potash applied at the rate of 2 or 3 oz. per square yard will assist in ripening and hardening the wood, if lightly forked in at the same time as the leavings of the mulch put down in May.

On over-acid soil a sprinkling of 2 oz. to the square yard of ground chalk will correct any excess acidity.

These are but a few suggestions, it being clearly impossible for me to give a detailed programme to suit all manner of soils, each requiring particular fare. If top-quality blooms are wanted, both organic matter and chemical fertiliser should be included in the diet.

Foliar Feeding

Foliar feeding, by means of a proprietary liquid feed obtainable especially for this purpose and applied with a syringe on the surface and underside of the leaves from June onwards, when the foliage has become mature, is becoming fashionable.

Murphy's Foliar Feed is recommended but not all rosarians are convinced that the new method is better than orthodox feeding, and find it, on the whole, harder work. Meanwhile, it is a mistake to think that it eliminates the need for soil improvement.

Whatever the method, feeding should stop in July for growth made later in the year is unlikely to survive winter conditions and is therefore a waste of the plant's vitality.

However, some gardeners like to give their roses a taste of sulphate of potash in August, as already suggested (about 2 to 3 oz. to the square yard) to assist the wood in ripening and enable it to stand up to the winter. The application is particularly helpful in areas with a heavy rainfall.

I should perhaps stress the point that over-feeding is a mistake and that an over-dose of fertiliser one month and none the next gives poor results.

The best and easiest way to feed the rose is by feeding the soil before planting. The proof that you are treating your roses correctly will be clear for all to see – healthy, firm and mature growth.

Watering

Mulching conserves moisture and will save the gardener laborious watering. However, during a drought of a fortnight or more on sandy or chalky soils, the roses will develop a real thirst. Newly-planted should be given a drink earlier than this: at regular weekly intervals in dry weather. If the soil around the plant has been covered with a mulch, this material must of course be drawn back to water the plants effectively.

If there are a number of bushes then an overhead sprinkler giving a fine spray is a boon. A hose fitted with a coarse nozzle is to be avoided, and a mist-like spray is the ideal. Dribs and drabs wetting the bed an inch deep do more harm than good, bringing the plants' roots to the surface where they may be burnt by the sun and encouraging cracks in hard baked soil. Cracks in the soil should be filled, so far as is possible, with granulated peat watered in with the aid of a garden hose or watering-can.

The gardener should aim at thoroughly soaking the mulch and top eight inches of soil early enough in the day for the foliage to dry before nightfall. If only a few roses are grown, it is of course preferable to use rainwater from a storage tank than water from a tap.

Roses grown against walls are frequently parched dry in March and April when rainfall is low and, sheltered from the elements as they are, may go desert-dry although the surrounding ground be soaking. Water from a can or hose often runs off the hard surface soil in the wrong direction and out of the reach of the roses' roots.

A 5-inch pot sunk into the soil 15 to 17 inches from the stem of each plant and kept regularly filled with water will supply moisture direct to the roots.

Ramblers should be grown in positions where air can circulate freely as they are particularly susceptible to disease.

Disbudding

Roses, even hybrid teas, have a habit of throwing a cluster of buds, the number varying according to the variety. If these are all left to mature, the blooms are likely to be of poor quality. If the hybrid tea is to be allowed to do itself credit the side buds should all be removed leaving the central bud and possibly the side bud that usually comes just below the cluster to develop.

Such roses should be disbudded at an early stage when the stalks of the buds are tender, the greatest care being taken not to damage the brittle neck of the central bud.

Floribundas do not require the same attention, but discreet thinning, removing an unwanted bud here and there to prevent overcrowding. If the crown bud is removed from the spray the remaining ones will open almost simultaneously, giving a more even performance.

The newly-planted must not be allowed to flower too generously for it is important that their energy should be conserved until they are really well established.

Disbudding is a rewarding attention but not an altogether essential one.

Dead-Heading

After flowering the faded heads must be removed so that the topmost outward-facing bud can develop. If the bud has not yet made its appearance then the gardener should cut back to the first leaf with five leaflets pointing away from the centre of the plant.

A large basket or bucket is needed when dead-heading the profuse floribundas. Harden your heart and decapitate as soon as the flowers fade, cutting back to a plump bud. In the case of the hybrid tea, the leaf-bud below the flower is often pointed and weak rather than flat and the gardener must cut back further, to a plump specimen capable of providing a good bloom further down the stem.

Exhibition roses need more severe treatment.

Below: Before and after disbudding a hybrid tea rose. This is done while the stalks of the buds are still tender

Cutting out growth which has carried flowers. This routine job should be carried out frequently in summer

Cutting Flowers

Newly-planted roses should be treated kindly, growth being of primary importance. Flowers wanted for the house should not be cut with long stalks during the first year.

Most rosarians like to cut their blooms early in the morning but some American researchers declare that roses gathered at noon in the sun last better than those picked at other times. The latest school of thought is that more harm than good is done by pounding the stems with a hammer or splitting and peeling them before putting them in water; the bruising and softening up of the stems is an open invitation to bacterial growth. This may well be, for it is undoubtedly the bacterial growth blocking the extremity of the stems that causes early demises. As I have always disliked the job of dethorning and stem-stripping, I am happy to fall in with this view and give it up.

Boiled water at a tepid temperature is often recommended for vases but I have not found that its use results in flowers lasting longer. Some flower arrangers advise cutting stalks afresh every day and putting the stems back into fresh water but this chore, I fear, is unrewarding. My tip is to pick the flowers in the late afternoon, plunge them deep into a bucket immediately after cutting and arrange them the following morning. I believe Chrysal, available from the sundriesman and chain chemist, does help cut roses to survive longer.

An arrangement of the lovely pink, splashed carmine climber, Madame Gregoire Staechelin

Hybridizing

Some of the finest roses we possess have been raised by amateurs. Lovely Ena Harkness was given to us by the late Albert Norman, a diamond setter in Hatton Garden.

Hybridizing is a fascinating pastime and yet few amateurs enter the field, first because it requires the possession of a greenhouse (not necessarily heated) as our summers are seldom conducive to seed-pods ripening outdoors, and secondly because the work of the hybridist is best carried out during the morning when many rosarians are away from home.

However, with the tremendous increase of interest in greenhouses and growing plants under glass it is likely that the number of hybridists will multiply. Here are some of the facts:

The first year the cross is made; the second year the seedling is 'budded' on to the rootstock; the third year the plant gives a full-sized flower. A decision may then be made to keep or discard the seedling. The fourth year, if the seedling is promising, it is sent to the Trial Grounds of the Royal National Rose Society at St. Albans, Hertfordshire, where it will stay under observation for two or three years. A Trial Ground Certificate *may* be won and a nurseryman be happy to distribute the variety. But he must first build up a stock and it may take him several more years to reach the stage when the rose can be introduced.

If the newcomer is really worthy, plant breeder's rights can be obtained and there is money to be made. It will be seen that the potential Gold Medal rose takes eight years or more to become a commercial success.

Choosing the Parents

The gardener must first choose two roses with known and desirable characteristics which he would wish to mate. Some growers have a flair for mating plants. Some have luck, some study genetics while others pick out two parents with the aid of a pin, and very often find themselves landed with the infertile.

The beginner who wishes to play safe should select reliable parents such as the hybrid teas Fragrant Cloud and Mischief.

Few roses have all the good qualities, one desirable characteristic seemingly cancelling out some shortcoming and vice versa. Awards made by the Royal National Rose Society are based on the following points:

Growth (vigour)	..	10 points
Habit of growth	..	10 points
Freedom from disease	..	20 points
Beauty of form and/or garden value	.. ..	10 points
Colour	.. .. ..	10 points
Freedom and continuity of flowering	.. ..	20 points
General effect	.. ..	10 points
Fragrance	.. ..	10 points

} 100 points

Freedom from disease is all-important and rosarians are on their knees praying for disease-resistant varieties, neither cursed by mildew nor bedevilled by black spot.

The flower, its colour and continuity of flowering are equally important. Vigour and health are essential but are by no means synonymous with lush, ugly or coarse growth.

The beginner has the difficult task of assessing the desirability of some of the glorious red roses that have unfortunate weak necks, yet superb damask scent. It is a problem to get all the blessings.

The less popular hard pinks, among them Wendy Cussons, by no means favourites in the garden, have the strong, sturdy necks that every hybridist is looking for. The short-petalled have many good points and the reds that die blue and badly are usually gloriously bright at their zenith and have a scent second to none. Unfortunately, the roses with well-defined, central-pointed cones often have disappointing foliage.

HYBRIDISTS' AMBITIONS

We are still looking for the perfect pink rose and the bright red rose with dark markings and an upright neck. There are some that want a blue rose, and the flower arrangers are now calling for the brown chrysanthemum shades while conservatives dream of hybrid teas and floribundas of the dark wine and black-purple shades freely available in the old-fashioned roses.

No doubt we shall get them but there is a great deal of work to be done before they make their appearance, even though many new seedlings are raised year by year.

As far as I am concerned, I would give the beginner carte blanche. Whatever his choice, and whatever the result, he will have achieved a new rose, unique and entirely his own even if it does not make him a millionaire.

The Marriage

The chosen parents should be brought into the greenhouse in December. They are best planted in the greenhouse border rather than in pots as this facilitates watering. The soil should not be over-rich as lush growth is to be avoided and on no account must the plants be fed with nitrogenous manure or fertilisers.

Watering should be fairly regular until June and then gradually reduced. June is usually a good month for making the cross and a warm bright day should be chosen.

The rose has both male and female organs (it is bisexual) so that the hybridist must decide which of his two selected roses is to be the seed-parent. One must be treated as seed or female, and the other as the pollen or male parent but there is nothing against reversing their positions if a second cross is to be made.

PREPARING THE FLOWERS

Ripe pollen must be taken from the anther of the male to the stigma or stigmas of the female at a time when the flowers of the female parent are open and the stigma in a sticky and receptive condition. To simplify the exercise the petals should be carefully taken away in their entirety, leaving no suspicion of a petal behind to cause decay.

The stamens on the seed parent (the male organs of the flower, of which the anthers form part) must be cut away for fear they should shed their pollen and so render cross-fertilization of no avail. (Some hybridists prefer to remove the stamens before the petals): this service is known as emasculation. As a further precaution, the prepared flower should be covered with a polythene bag to prevent its pistils being fertilized by any busy pollen-carrying insect and to allow them to mature in safety.

After 24 hours during a hot spell, or as long as two or three days during a cold period, the pistils become sticky and ready to receive the pollen. The male parent selected for pollen should now be picked from the plant, the stamens cut off (quite a tricky business) and laid in a small glass dish where within a few hours they will drop off their pollen.

The pollen can now be lifted with a camel-hair brush and applied carefully to the waiting pistil. The brush should be sterilised in alcohol after each operation when carrying out a series of crosses between different parents. This work should be done when the house has reached a warm temperature. Alternatively, the method shown on p. 52 may be used.

RIPENING THE SEED

When the seed parent is labelled with the name of the male there is nothing more to be done until November (except for routine watering) when the hep which results from a successful cross should have coloured and swelled and be ready for picking. It should be cut off with at least 2 inches of stalk and placed in a pan of damp sand, peat or vermiculite and left until the beginning of February, when the seed is removed from the pods and sown.

Most rosarians suggest that the seed should spend this ripening period outside, in a position with a northern aspect and protected from pests such as field mice and grey squirrels. Professionals seem to prefer to ripen the seed meticulously in a steady temperature of 60°F.

Seed Sowing

In February the seed is sown about $\frac{1}{2}$ to 1 inch deep and 2 inches apart in pots or boxes. Sterilized soil of the John Innes formula is best used with a generous sprinkling of coarse sand, and if possible a temperature around 55° to 60°F. should be maintained, although heat is not essential.

Seedlings should begin to appear during March and April but the time of germination varies and hybrid teas may not show themselves until late

Hybridization. The bloom (above left) is at the correct stage of development for use as a seed parent. The petals (above right) and the stamens surrounding the stigmas (below left) are removed carefully. After 24 hours or longer the stigmas will be sticky and ready to receive the pollen (below right)

summer. When the seedlings have formed true leaves, they may be lifted and transferred to boxes or be given individual pots. They will flower in May or June and the useless, the papery, five-petalled, dirty-coloured and worthless can often be scrapped straightaway.

Once the unwanted have been removed the remaining 'possibles' or, if fortunate, 'promising' or even 'probables' should be well cared for – sprayed with colloidal sulphur against mildew, with captan against damping off and with malathion against greenfly.

In the second year the buds from the seedlings can be budded onto prepared rootstocks, usually Rugosa. This is not very easy for the seedling plants, of course, are of small size and the buds to be removed are in proportion. The bud is cut from the seedling with a sharp knife and, unlike ordinary budding described in the following chapter, the wood behind the bud it left intact. It is then inserted into the 'T' shaped incision made in the back of the rootstock and if competently positioned will quite quickly start into growth. (See budding p. 53.)

It is in the third year that the full-sized flower presents itself and an assessment of the flower made. Hopes will surely rise and fall and assessments will be made and re-made many times from now onwards. The world-famous hybridist Mr Wilhelm Kordes explained to me the many difficulties of making these assessments at every stage, and, of course, no judgment is fair until the variety has shown its worth when grown outside.

The amateur hybridist will no doubt discard some of his budded seedlings while re-budding the hopefuls, and good-luck to him.

A million new seedlings are raised every year and it is my hope that this chapter, an over-simplification of an art, will encourage the reader to raise the number to at least a million and one even if the odds are against him.

Propagation

Roses are propagated by seeds, cuttings and budding. They can also be grafted but this method, requiring heat and an expert's hand, is best left to the professional.

Seed

The ancestry of the modern hybrid tea is mixed indeed and seed from a plant in a gardener's rose bed is likely to produce a poor thing with little resemblance to the bush it came from. Rose species will, of course, give a more satisfactory return.

Because of the disappointing results obtained from raising hybrid teas and floribundas from seed obtained from natural crosses the rosarian relies on hybridization for new varieties (see Hybridizing, pp. 50 to 52).

Cuttings

Cuttings are an easy way of propagating roses, and the plants that result have the one advantage of being free from troublesome suckers, but, alas, they seldom possess the vigour of the budded plant and not all varieties are willing to strike from a twig stuck in the ground, even with the help of a hormone powder. The yellow and the modern Super-Star-coloured varieties seldom make the effort.

The beginner wishing to try his hand should start in August or September with the red or pink rambler, or failing these a vigorous floribunda.

PREPARING CUTTINGS

Ripe shoots of early summer's growth should be cut $\frac{1}{4}$ inch below the lower eye. The cutting should then be trimmed at the top if longer than a foot, reducing it to 9 or 10 inches by making a slanting cut just above an eye as in pruning and leaving the two or three topmost leaves and removing the rest. The importance of using a sharp, clean knife cannot be overstressed.

The base of the cutting should now be dipped first in water and then in a rooting hormone powder to a depth of at least 1 inch. No. 2 Seradix Powder is advised for the treatment of medium hard and No. 3 for hard wood cuttings.

A sheltered place in the garden not overhung by trees has now to be found and a trench of about 6 to 7 inches depth to be made. The bottom of the trench should be generously sprinkled with coarse sand; if the soil is dry is should be well watered, allowing the moisture to drain away before planting.

PLANTING

The cuttings should be firmly planted, 6 inches apart, with two-thirds of their length below ground; this excessive-sounding depth is helpful in reducing the loss of moisture.

The protection of a frame or cloche will increase the chances of the cuttings' survival, but success will vary with the variety. Albertine and American Pillar are splendidly co-operative but the pithy-wooded hybrids often disappoint the most skilled rosarians.

By spring of the following year it will be possible to see whether the cuttings have rooted. They should be left where they are until the autumn when they will be ready for transplanting.

Finally, harden your heart with any weedy young plant; it seldom makes good and there are enough hypochondriacs in most gardens already.

Budding

Not all nurserymen agree as to the most desirable rootstock, understock, for budding and I have heard them arguing deep into the night on the suitability of different stocks for different soils and climate. However the majority agree that if good briars of *Rosa canina,* the old Dog Rose, are to be had and the garden is on rich heavy loam, then there is none better.

R. laxa gives sturdy plants and few suckers, and is at its best for this purpose during the early part of the summer when the sap is running fast. The heavily-thorned *R. multiflora,* sometimes known as *polyantha simplex,* should be considered by the gardener on poor soil. Cuttings of 9 to 10 inches in length can be taken from this stock and *R. canina* in September, these being prepared as described on p. 53. They should be ready for budding in the July or August following but there is some doubt whether stocks from such cuttings have as long a life as seedling stocks.

Meanwhile, *R. rugosa* is popular with nurserymen and is generally grown. It is cheap to produce, willing to bud, uniform in performance, splendidly vigorous and its fibrous roots flourish on light soil – it has one failing, a maddening habit of throwing suckers.

PLANTING ROOTSTOCKS

The gardener, having made his choice of understock to suit his soil, should plant his rootstocks 12 inches apart, allowing $2\frac{1}{2}$ feet between the rows.

The beginner's besetting sin is to plant the rootstocks too deeply, burying the neck where the root forks out. He must aim at keeping the neck above the level of the ground and so, when the time comes, facilitate budding.

There are several schools of thought about the treatment of the young-rooted stock. Exhibitors plant the stocks in permanent positions and bud them *in situ* but the home gardener without show bench ambitions usually treats the cuttings to at least one move to inspire the resulting plants to make fibrous roots and discourage those that are deep-diving.

No attempt should be made to bud during a drought, when the stocks may be at a standstill, without copious watering to start them into growth. On the other hand, over-vigorous growth that will 'drown' the bud is to be avoided.

INTRODUCING THE BUD

A professional budder, bent in two like a hairpin and with the aid of a second person – a 'tier' – following behind him, is capable of budding 1,500 stocks a day. The ungainly position which must be taken up by the budder for long stretches makes this an occupation suitable only for the young. Those with disc trouble must adapt themselves by kneeling on one knee, or even two, and using a kneeling pad.

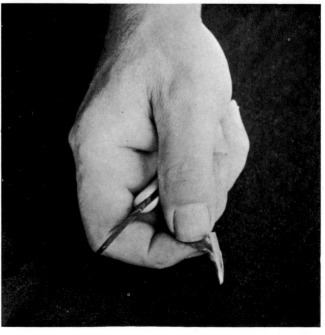

Budding roses. The bud is removed carefully with a sharp knife (above). The sliver of wood behind the bud is removed (below) and the shield (bottom picture) trimmed for insertion in the prepared rootstock

In July or August the shoots that provide the buds are gathered. The better quality the budding knife used subsequently the easier the job. It must be kept razor-sharp: a strop or rub on an emery paper tool stick is necessary, the blade being in contact with sap from the plant. The wedge-shaped handle that serves to open the bark of the stock must also be kept hospital clean.

Select a shoot from the variety chosen for budding which has a first-class fading flower and remove it before the thorns have dried and hardened. The leaves should then be trimmed off but the leaf stalk left as it is handy for holding the bud shield.

A T-shaped incision is made in the stock. The bark is carefully lifted back (above) and the bud shield slipped into place (below). The bud is then tied securely, with raffia (see right) or adhesive tape

Another requirement is a supply of best raffia of $\frac{1}{4}$ inch width cut to lengths of 20 inches. The raffia should be soaked in water and softened up before use. Special rubber patches and adhesive tape are to be had for budding and these have the advantage of stretching as the stem grows.

INSERTING THE BUD SHIELD

Ready for action, the soil can now be scraped away from the base of the stock, the neck wiped clean and a cross cut made $\frac{3}{4}$ inch above the forking of the roots; the cut should be deep enough to penetrate the bark but no more. The second cut should start $\frac{3}{4}$ inch below the first: it should be an upright incision that on meeting the first cut, completes a T shape. Then, with the wedge-shaped handle of the knife, lift back the bark without tearing it to prepare for the introduction of the bud shield.

With standard roses, of course, the bud is secured on the lateral growth at the head, very near to the main stem (see Making a Standard Rose, pp 108 and 109).

Now taking the bud-stick in the left hand prepare the bud shield for insertion by placing the knife-blade about ½ inch under the bud and scoop it out, afterwards slicing away the sliver of wood left behind the bud. This operation is often found the most pernickety of the performance as the bud must be left with enough surrounding bark to ensure its safety. The shield is trimmed so that it can be slipped comfortably into the T cut in the stock. Holding it by the leaf-stalk there should be no difficulty in easing it in. Then, folding back the bark, the bud can be firmly tied in.

If raffia is used the bud should be by-passed, bandaging from the bottom up and giving the raffia two turns below the bud and three above before completion. If adhesive tape is used the bud may be bandaged over and be relied upon to make its way through the tape. The leaf-stalk, now of no further use, may be cut back to the stem.

Two or three buddings can be made at different stations on the stem and there are adventurous rosarians who like to bud two or three different varieties on the one stem, an attractive idea that seldom works out. As in the case of the family fruit tree carrying three or four varieties of apples, the strongest of the competitors takes over and the more delicate are rarely given the chance of putting up a show.

The deed done, on bush roses the soil can now be drawn back to the level of the bud. If successful, the growing tissues will develop fast, and the stem will freshen in colour after a few months; if the bud shield turns brown it is hoped the gardener will manfully face defeat and try again.

On occasions, a swelling develops below the bud where the tie has been too tight: a careful easing of the raffia should put the matter right.

LATER ATTENTIONS

When February comes and the severe frosts are over, all rootstocks should be headed-back or cut away beyond the bud, but not too close to risk damage to the bud. It is wise to paint the wound with copper-based fungicide and so reduce the risk of canker. The stem should be tied to a cane for a year or so for safety's sake.

In a wet season the ties will rot off in two months; if still in place and strangling the stem after this period, they are best removed. When the new growth reaches 5 or 6 inches in length it may be pinched back to encourage eyes to break into growth. The plant will flower through the summer, and when winter comes the new bush can take its place in border or bed.

I realise from experience that budding routine on paper is difficult to follow but happily once seen and practised it is as easy as pie to at least understand if not to carry out.

Sports or Mutations

From time to time an entirely new break in colour or form will make its appearance on an established species or variety – this is known as a mutation or sport and is a freak of nature.

In the same way, a bush may suddenly develop climbing characteristics and we have sports to thank for many of our roses; Alison Wheatcroft is a sport of Circus, Climbing Lady Sylvia is a sport of Lady Sylvia and so on.

Any variation from the normal can be termed a sport; mutation is the scientific name for the variation. The sporting follows a change in one or more genes within the chromosomes.

Sports are perpetuated by propagating material from the sporting shoot and once plants of the new form have been established cuttings can be taken freely from the plant.

Part Two

Hybrid Teas
Floribundas
Climbers
Polyantha or Poly-Pompons
Miniature Roses
Roses Under Glass
Exhibiting

I would now like to bring to the gardener's notice roses that, in my opinion, deserve his attention and to assist him in his buying. The list of roses given is by no means complete but merely a selection and the fact that a rose is not mentioned should not be taken as a reflection on its reputation.

Hybrid Teas

It is increasingly difficult to classify roses for many of the floribundas are growing in size and becoming border-line hybrid teas. However, in spite of the challenge of the floribunda the hybrid tea holds pride of place in our gardens and has reigned supreme since the appearance of the silvery-pink heavily-scented La France in 1867.

The modern hybrid tea is nearly always double, has large, shapely flowers of many petals and normally a single bloom of splendid substance. The buds are pointed and the plant of pleasing bushy growth; the rose of today has shown itself to be freer flowering and less sensitive to climate than its predecessor. The blooms come in flushes with a resting period between the bursts.

The hybrid tea list is a long one for it includes the hybrid perpetuals, hybrid teas, teas and pernetianas. Of these earlier types, Frau Karl Druschki (introduced in 1900) is still the best large white, and apricot-yellow Lady Hillingdon (1910) still survives if mainly for sentimental reasons, while bright crimson Hugh Dickson (1904), pegged down as seen at Sissinghurst Castle in the days of Victoria Sackville-West, can be superb and is heavily fragrant.

Few hybrid teas with their mixed pedigrees maintain their high standard of performance after 20 years or so. Even Peace with its incomparable vigour is said to be on the slippery slope, due, no doubt, to certain nurserymen budding eyes of poor stock.

Keen rosarians untroubled by nostalgia should turn to the new varieties, in particular those which have received the awards of the Royal National Rose Society's Trial Ground Certificate or Gold Medal, or the American 'AARS', the All America Rose Selections test garden certificate – guarantees of the highest order.

Above: *Ernest H. Morse*

Above: *Super Star*

Right: *Madame Louis Laperrière*.
Far right: *Papa Meilland*

Above: *Josephine Bruce*

Red

ENA HARKNESS: scarlet with deep red shading, is outstanding and often of exhibition size. The heavy flowers hang their heads in dry weather but if well fed and kept moist the tendency to nod can be overcome.

ERNEST H. MORSE: turkey-red with plentiful dark green foliage and a sweet scent: has a reputation for being resistant to disease.

FRAGRANT CLOUD: dusky scarlet; is not my favourite colour but is a fine rose and beautifully fragrant.

JOSEPHINE BRUCE: a good scarlet overlaid with black-maroon, with smallish flowers of perfect shape. A velvety fragrant rose that must be watched for mildew.

KONRAD ADENAUER: a clear red; is useful for exhibition.

MADAME LOUIS LAPERRIÈRE: a profuse scarlet shaded maroon, and an excellent bedding rose.

PAPA MEILLAND: dark crimson and heavily scented. First-rate under glass but must be watched for mildew.

SUPER STAR: the successful luminous vermillion; a universal favourite and borderline floribunda.

UNCLE WALTER: a large, vigorous, brilliant crimson rose, perhaps more of a shrub than a bedder.

WENDY CUSSONS: a strong fine rose of cerise-red with generous foliage. The high-pointed blooms have a heavenly scent. Wendy is difficult to fault.

The reds chosen are beautifully fragrant. Splendid dark red Chrysler Imperial is omitted as it fades 'blue'.

Wendy Cussons

Eden Rose

Above: *Silver Lining*

Pink

ANNE LETTS: a clear silvery-pink; shy but recommended to the exhibitor.

EDEN ROSE: a two-toned pink, slightly scented, of exhibition size that stands up well to bad weather.

GAIL BORDEN: a large deep peach with a golden reverse; a splendid exhibition flower. Perfect for cutting but only slightly scented.

GAVOTTE: light rose-pink with pale reverse. An ideal exhibition flower.

HELEN TRAUBEL: pale salmon-pink with sweet fragrance: always spectacular in Queen Mary's Garden, Regents Park, London.

Above: *Helen Traubel*

Below: *Margaret*

MARGARET: a clear pink Irish rose of perfect form; many petalled and vulnerable to the rain. Fragrant.

MISCHIEF: a coral-salmon pink; an excellent garden rose with slight fragrance.

MY CHOICE: pale carmine and buff with gold buds splashed crimson; a first-rate bedder, vigorous and free-flowering.

OPHELIA (introduced 1912): this variety and its progeny Madame Butterfly and Lady Sylvia are still well-loved and almost as free-flowering as a floribunda. A trio of pink-salmon flowers with a delicious clean scent.

PERFECTA: a large light rose-pink shading paler; a trifle 'rough' at the beginning of the season but an

Stella

Above: *Pink Peace*

Below: *Mischief*

outstanding rose if it is given a good summer.

PINK FAVOURITE: inner petals shell-pink, outer petals a deeper shade. A healthy garden or exhibition rose, profuse but only slightly scented.

PINK PEACE: deep pink. Has size and sweet scent but bears little resemblance to its famous predecessor, Peace (see p. 65).

PINK SUPREME: lovely pink, paler at the edges; moderately full and flattish with large fragrant flowers. One of the Superintendent's favourites in Queen Mary's Garden, Regent's Park.

PREMIER BAL: cyclamen flowers ivory-edged; a romantic rose but not an ideal bedder, given to balling-up in the rain. Deserves a place in the garden but not a bed to itself.

PRIMA BALLERINA: cherry pink; wet-summer stand-by of lovely shape with rich scent and winning golden stamens. Reliable and fragrant.

ROSE GAUJARD: a deep pink with silvery reverse and bright green foliage. It stands up to the rain; a gallant subject often willing to grow where other varieties fail.

SILVER LINING: a pale pink-silver, high-pointed, elegant and scented flower.

STELLA: a large rounded bloom with a cream-blush centre surrounded by deep pink petals. A healthy exhibitor's plant but seldom a generous flowerer.

61

Right: *The hybrid tea variety Gail Borden (see p. 60)*

Below: *The hybrid tea variety My Choice (see p. 60)*

Far right: *The hybrid tea variety King's Ransom, arranged by Sheila Macqueen (see p. 65)*

Orange

BEAUTE: deep apricot shaded red; great distinction and beauty. Abundant deep green foliage. Only slightly fragrant.

BETTINA: flaming orange with a golden base. Fragrant; pleasant bronzy foliage.

MOJAVE: deep orange, shaded and veined carmine. Good glossy foliage. A striking and excellent bedding plant, richly scented.

MONTEZUMA: deep orange-salmon, well formed and free. Plentiful foliage: slightly fragrant. Sad and sorry in the rain.

MRS SAM MCGREDY (introduced 1929): bright orange-copper to scarlet; still a highlight in roses, if not quite so robust as the moderns.

SORAYA: an orange-flame, darker on outer petals. Large, full, fragrant and free-flowering.

Above: *Mojave*   Below: *Bettina*

Yellow

BUCCANEER: clear golden-yellow; moderate size and of tea fragrance. A vigorous, tall-growing plant with dark, leathery foliage. Must be cleverly placed or it may swamp its neighbours.

DOROTHY PEACH: yellow flushed red in bud, opening to yellow edged buff; a lovely bedding rose.

GRAND'MÈRE JENNY: golden-yellow with peach shading. Free, vigorous and upright and slightly fragrant.

GRANDPA DICKSON (introduced 1966): lemon, fading to cream-yellow. A comparative new-comer of which I warily take a happy view. Leathery, disease-resistant foliage. Alas, little scent.

KING'S RANSOM: a clear pale yellow. An All America Rose Selections Winner with high-centred blooms and a fair fragrance; lively and healthy – a welcome addition to the colour group.

MCGREDY'S YELLOW (introduced 1933): buttercup yellow. Still one of the best and deservedly given a place in the majority of rose gardens. Excellent bedder branching freely, but the large flower is vulnerable to weather. Fragrant.

PEACE: deep yellow stained cerise-pink on the outer edges of the petals. Rightly known as the rose of the century. At times described as a little 'coarse' but a magnificient variety that one hesitates to criticise. It should be only lightly pruned and when possible allowed to become a large shrub.

SPEK'S YELLOW: an exceptional deep golden-yellow; small, well-shaped flowers. Tall but inclined to straggle.

SUTTER'S GOLD: rich old gold; long, distinguished blooms, perfect for cutting. A first-rate bedder with a fruity fragrance.

Buccaneer

Dorothy Peach

Below: *Grandpa Dickson*

White

FRAU KARL DRUSCHKI (introduced 1900): a pure dead white from carmine stained buds. Does equally well as Hugh Dickson when pegged down. Our best white, but, alas, scentless.

MESSAGE: a fuller flower than its competitor Virgo. Fragrant and free, it is vulnerable to mildew and rain.

PASCALI: well-shaped and moderately full. Is usually mildew free and the best white rose for cold areas.

VIRGO: creamy-white: probably the most popular of the whites, and undoubtedly the best of the group for bedding. Vulnerable to mildew in the autumn.

Bicolour or Polychrome

PICCADILLY: the most striking bicolour of the century; vivid geranium-lake with a golden reverse. A profuse and brilliant performer and fragrant into the bargain.

TZIGANE: another scarlet and gold and probably a better exhibition flower than Piccadilly. Vigorous, upright, slightly fragrant and with glossy copper beech-coloured foliage: it makes an excellent bedder.

Lilac

BLUE MOON: ice blue. The plant produces a few flowers of great size.

INTERMEZZO: silvery-blue with good foliage.

LILAC TIME: lavender-pink flowers of moderate size. Slightly fragrant.

STERLING SILVER: silver-blue and as yet the best in colour of the group and with the best scent. By no means robust, the plant benefits by disbudding and grows well under glass. Decorative and charming.

The lilacs are not truly 'blue,' but I understand that there are some exciting new introductions to be made in the near future.

An exhibitor's display of Frau Karl Druschki

Piccadilly

Floribundas

The floribunda is the perpetual cluster rose that flowers throughout the summer. Some varieties are, of course, more continuous flowering than others but there is, as a rule, a secondary shoot and bloom positioned below the main flower head ready to take over before the main bloom has faded.

This is a madly floriferous labour-saver, maybe taking a short rest from time to time between bursts, but very nearly as continuous flowering as a bedding plant. It is not surprising that it now plays an important part in the summer garden and has come to stay.

Poulsen of Denmark was responsible for developing the Poulsen group that are the forerunners of the race. He was looking for a hardier subject than the hybrid tea, more suitable to his cold climate and set to work crossing the polyanthas, naming many of them after members of his family. As he progressed other hybridists, recognising the potential of the Poulsen blood, stepped in.

The smaller flowers have not as yet the individual beauty or refinement of the hybrid tea but they have the tremendous advantage of being disease resistant. This resistance is said to be due to their being more closely related to the species. Added to this they are remarkably hardy and unaffected by the severest of frosts.

Certain varieties fall short of the usual resistance and Fashion is often reported as suffering from rust although many rosarians have grown it for years and found it trouble-free. Frensham, however, is undeniably mildew-prone, and more the pity for it is a lovely matt-crimson hedge-maker and one of the best floribundas we possess.

When it comes to colours there are the 'hot' and brash, the brilliant and exciting, the vermillion screamers and others as shrill beside the pastels, soft pinks, white and cream. There are also those that change from yellow to pink and on to red as they age such as the rather over-exposed Masquerade, Circus and Rumba.

The choice is wide and the varieties so numerous that there is difficulty in distinguishing one from another, particularly among the host of crimsons.

The modern gardener now looks for colour stability among his reds and yellows. Floribundas such as Korona fade fast to salmon and lovely Elizabeth of Glamis finishes badly. Others burn or bleach to unpleasant tints while the reds are given to blueing.

Colour stability is greatly influenced by soil, but there are some varieties that hold their colour more successfully than others, such as Evelyn Fison and Orange Sensation, and these are the ones to look for.

Red

AMA: bright scarlet, semi-double with large trusses and healthy foliage. An alternative to Frensham that is so vulnerable to mildew. Height, $2\frac{1}{2}$ feet.

ANNA WHEATCROFT: one of the first true vermilions; single or semi-single. Height, 2 feet.

CITY OF BELFAST: a splendid deep orange-vermilion and winner of the Royal National Rose Society's President's International Trophy for the best new seedling of 1967. Height, 3 to 4 feet.

DICKSON'S FLAME: the semi-double, flame-scarlet blooms do not burn or fade. One of the best for a mass effect. Height, 2 feet.

DUSKY MAIDEN: single or semi-single of darkest crimson with golden anthers. Quite sweetly scented. Height, 2 feet.

EVELYN FISON: pure red, semi-double flowers. A weather resistant bedding rose. Height, 3 feet.

FASHION: unique coral-salmon for industrial areas, free from rust. Height, 2 feet.

FRENSHAM: strong, semi-double matt-crimson that makes an outstanding hedge-maker. For mildew-free gardens only. Height 3 to 4 feet.

Orange Sensation, a light vermilion variety with many attributes (see p. 70)

Above: *Dickson's Flame (see p. 68)*

KORONA: brilliant orange-scarlet; a continuous flowerer but would seem to vary in its performance in different parts of the country. A good bad weather subject. Height, $3\frac{1}{2}$ feet.

LILLI MARLENE: bright crimson-scarlet that flowers well, holds its colour and is weather resistant; immensely popular. Height, $2\frac{1}{2}$ feet.

ORANGEADE: massive heads of brilliant luminous scarlet, single flowers that give a dazzling performance. Height, $2\frac{1}{2}$ feet.

ORANGE SENSATION: semi-double, light vermilion with many attributes – scent, a long-lasting flowering record, and healthy dark green foliage. Height, 2 to 3 feet.

PAPRIKA: poppy-red and sparkling with an almost purple centre; an excellent variety that does not fade. Height, $2\frac{1}{2}$ feet.

Evelyn Fison (see p. 68)

RED DANDY: first-rate dark-red floribunda of velvet texture and hybrid tea shape. Not quite as free flowering as the smaller type of blooms but should not be missed out. Resistant to mildew and useful in a garden where this trouble persists. Height, $2\frac{1}{2}$ feet.

Above: *Lilli Marlene*

Introduced in 1951, the Garnettes are now to be had in red, pink and yellow while small roses of the Garnette type in white, apricot and other new shades are on their way to Europe from America. The group has a great reputation for long-lasting cut flowers, often remaining fresh for 10 days. They are forcing roses widely grown on the Continent. Height, 1 foot.

ROSEMARY ROSE: double, rosy-red and delightful with deep green foliage and sweetly-scented. This is a flat-faced charmer but, alas, the tinged-copper foliage is vulnerable to mildew. Height, 2 to $2\frac{1}{2}$ feet.

SARABANDE: vivid, unfading orange-red, semi-double, with pleasing deep green foliage. This is a good continuous-flowering bedding rose. Height, 2 to $2\frac{1}{2}$ feet.

Rosemary Rose

RED FAVOURITE: small dark-red rosette flowering variety with a neat habit. Reliable and useful where a short bedder is wanted. Height, 1 foot.

RED GARNETTE: the Garnettes, with small rosette-shaped blooms, are very free-flowering varieties which are better under glass than out of doors.

Multicolour

Paint Box

This tri-colour freak performance with golden buds opening salmon and deepening to crimson began with Masquerade. Here are four that cleverly change their make-up for those who enjoy the conjuring trick:

CIRCUS: neat, very free-flowering, sturdy and upright but not suitable for cold exposed gardens. Height, 2 feet.

MASQUERADE: flowers yellow, salmon and pink simultaneously, and seen everywhere. A striking performer that created a new fashion in floribundas, gay and bright but by no means a distinguished flower. Height, 3 feet.

PAINT BOX: in the opinion of some an improved Masquerade. The red and deep yellow petals change to deep red as they age. Height, $3\frac{1}{2}$ feet.

REDGOLD: this is an attractive newcomer. The gold merges into red at the edges and the bloom fades to peach or orange. Foliage dark green and plant of medium height. It claims 'moderate' fragrance.

Below: *Masquerade*

Sir Lancelot

Apricot

SIR LANCELOT: a welcome semi-double, apricot-yellow. Vigorous if a little irregular in growth and weather resistant but must be watched for black spot and mildew. Height, 2 feet.

WOBURN ABBEY is a glorious tangerine-apricot and ZAMBRA a desirable orange with golden reverse but, alas, the former has indifferent health and the latter requires better summers than we get.

Yellow

ALLGOLD: a splendid, clear and unfading deep yellow, a 1956 introduction that is unsurpassed. The glossy foliage is remarkably free from black spot. Starting to flower early, it blooms on until the frost. A wonderful bedder. Height, 2 to 2½ feet.

CHINATOWN: tough and hardy with deep yellow blooms; this variety should perhaps be listed as a shrub. It flowers exuberantly but should be kept to the shrubbery or border and not the bed. Height 4 to 6 feet.

Above: *Redgold, an attractive new floribunda rose. It is of medium height*

Far right: *Iceberg, a vigorous, free-flowering and outstanding floribunda rose, arranged by Sheila Macqueen*

Right: *Goldgleam*

GOLDGLEAM: excellent clear deep lemon-yellow with plentiful glossy small foliage and some scent. Raised by Mr E. B. LeGrice who gave us Allgold. Height, $2\frac{1}{2}$ to 3 feet.

HONEYMOON: a Kordes charmer; a canary-yellow paling towards the margins. Flowers on when others are over. Tall and unsuited for bedding. Height, 3 feet.

Above: *Dearest*

Far left: *Sea Pearl*

Left: *The buds of Sea Pearl are elegant, long and tapered*

Pink

DEAREST: large, semi-double salmon-pink and very free flowering. Perfect for bedding this is one of the best floribundas we possess and my favourite. Height, 2 to 3 feet.

ELIZABETH OF GLAMIS: another salmon-pink of distinction. Weather resistant, it flowers freely and is a healthy and beautiful plant but its blooms finish badly. Height, 2½ to 3 feet.

PADDY MCGREDY: borderline floribunda with hybrid tea-sized flowers of carmine-pink. It takes a little time to recover from the first profuse flush of bloom and is therefore an intermittent performer that should be used in a border rather than as a bedding plant. Slightly scented. Height, 2 feet.

PLENTIFUL: fully double, flat blooms of a delightful pink. This rose has great charm and should not be missed. Height, 2 feet.

QUEEN ELIZABETH: a superb pink variety but inclined to grow tall. An excellent variety for hedge making. Height, up to 6 feet.

SEA PEARL: hybrid tea type of bloom of a clear pink suffused gold. This floribunda has the most elegant long and pointed buds and is altogether a distinctive and delicate variety that would seem to have been overlooked or under-rated. Height, 3 to 4 feet.

Lilac

AFRICA STAR: fully double, mauve, large flowers and coppery foliage. Moderately vigorous and vulnerable to black spot. Height, $1\frac{1}{2}$ feet.

Lilac Charm

LILAC CHARM: a clear lilac single flower with golden anthers. A rose I enjoy growing. Height, 2 feet.

MAGENTA: fully double of rosette-form with an old fashioned look. Vigorous and needs to be pruned into place. Height, $2\frac{1}{2}$ to 3 feet.

OVERTURE: purplish-mauve with blooms of hybrid tea type with decorative golden anthers. Height, 1 to $1\frac{1}{2}$ feet.

Africa Star

Magenta

White

ICEBERG: surely heads the list of desirable, vigorous and free-flowering floribundas. The buds are tinted pink and the flowers slightly scented – a first-rate bedding rose. Height, 3 to $3\frac{1}{2}$ feet.

IVORY FASHION: semi-double, off-white, particularly free-flowering towards the end of the season. The matt foliage is moderately vigorous; flowers have slight scent. Height, $1\frac{1}{2}$ to 2 feet.

Elizabeth of Glamis, a distinguished, fragrant, weather-resistant floribunda
(see p. 76)

Paddy McGredy, a floribunda with hybrid tea-sized flowers
(see p. 77)

Above and below: *Queen Elizabeth, a tall floribunda excellent for hedge-making*
(see p. 77)

Climbers

The mixed ancestry of the climbers makes it almost impossible to classify them; they are even more inter-married than the hybrid teas. In the hope of helping the reader, I have divided them into five groups: climbing sports, vigorous climbing roses of the hybrid tea type, perpetual-flowering climbers, ramblers and wichuraianas, and scrambling species and hybrids.

Perhaps it should be stressed that the more free-flowering the climber the less vigorous and tall-growing it is likely to be and that the very strong climbers are not suited for light arches or restricted space on house or wall, but are best kept to large, strong screens where they are free to roam fancy free.

Climbers should, whenever possible, be planted in the autumn and certainly before Christmas as they carry considerable top-growth that demands much of the newly-planted unless well-rooted.

The new arrivals benefit from overhead spraying with water during dry periods in spring and summer until established.

A decorative rose pergola. The great veteran, pink Climbing Madame Caroline Testout (see p. 86)
Right: *The golden-yellow, semi-double climber Golden Showers (see p. 88)*

Framework and Supports

THE PERGOLA

This is a foliage or flower-covered walk. The wise gardener builds his pergola to last and outlive him. The supports for the climbers at sides and overhead can be of any material provided they can stand the weight and wind.

Brick pillars of 14 inches or more in width are the ideal, keeping the walk wide so that the roses can grow freely without getting in the way of the passer-by. Wooden cross-bars, poles treated with a preservative, chains or coir cords can be used to connect the tops. Should timber posts be used they can be strengthened by driving in thin galvanised pipes at their base to reinforce them.

A pergola furnished with Kordesii varieties or different ramblers is a great glory for five or six weeks in the summer, and a cool walk when out of flower on a hot summer's day. The Wichuraiana variety Albertine is renowned for covering any obstacle in a few seasons but the complaint is growing that it flowers but once a year when there are many these days that give a recurrent or repeat performance.

The object of the pergola is, of course, that it should lead somewhere – to a gazebo, seat, or perhaps a statue or fountain or just another part of the garden. Without such an object it loses purpose.

ARCHWAYS

Are excellent for framing a view or feature or for providing an element of surprise. An opening in a wall surrounded with climbing roses makes an effective porthole; it can also be an amusing peephole between a classical and wild garden.

PILLARS AND STATUARY

Pillars of marble, brick, cement, prefabricated material or wood are very helpful in supporting climbing roses of the less exuberant type, reaching 10 feet.

WALLS

The climber looks at its best against an old brick wall. Ugly walls can be greatly improved and lightened by being painted or whitewashed: a light coat is all that is needed and should the shape of the bricks show through, so much the better. New and brash red bricks can also be toned down in a similar manner.

Trellis, wide-meshed netting fixed in panels or, better still, parallel wires, are called for if the roses are to grow to any height. Miss H. Murrell of Portland Nurseries, Shrewsbury suggest that when there is any length of wall to be covered, pig netting, unrolled horizontally along the wall, with the lower edge about 3 feet from the ground, is highly successful.

Climbers grown on the house are best provided with a trellis to the first floor, above which wires should be organised to which the roses can be fastened. The installation of the necessary vine eyes for the wires is not easy and requires particular tools and a skilled hand.

SCREENS

Protection from prying eyes is much needed in suburban gardens, and when brick and stone cannot be afforded trellis, wattle or osier hurdles must take their place. The lighter growing the roses chosen as a covering for these, the longer the screen will last.

The introduction of pre-cast pierced concrete blocks, U-, V- or fancy-shaped ridge tiles and so on, has provided the gardener with useful and decorative dividing walls and a protection from neighbours and winds. The claire-voie pattern will be found adequate by all but the sensitive sun-bather shy of peeping-toms.

Pillar roses in Queen Mary's Garden, Regent's Park, London

Above: *Training the rose Albertine on to a wire framework*

Left: *Albertine, flowering with gay abandon*

The glorious white climber Madame Alfred Carrière

TRIPODS

The modern and by far the best method of growing the rambler and the restrained climbing rose is on a 7-foot tripod. This makes pruning and tying easy and shows the rose off to best advantage.

TREES AS SUPPORTS

Shrubs and trees are the rose's natural support. Nothing looks more beautiful than the wild rose tumbling through a tall young hawthorn, or *R. moyesii* as I have seen it scrambling over two conifers simultaneously.

Acer platanoides Goldsworth Purple, with its rich deep purple foliage that persists the summer through, makes a flattering host for the single red climbing rose. Such a planting can be seen in the red border at Hidcote, Gloucestershire, one of the National Trust's most famous gardens.

Meanwhile, *R. filipes* will almost in a flash smother an old tree with its decorative pale green trails and fascinating clusters of white, yellow centred flowers. Or it will thread its way through a Scots pine and frock it like a lace-trimming.

There is no doubt the climbing rose shows off best when seen growing overhead.

COMPANIONS

The climbing rose makes a satisfactory support for other climbing plants, and in particular the clematis that really has no liking for making its ascent alone at the mercy of the wind.

Nellie Moser, Jackmanii and *C. montana* because of their willing nature are a trifle over-exposed. I would suggest planting the white, dark centred Henryii, or perhaps Marie Boisselot (sometimes known as Madame Le Coultre) with golden anthers; both climb lightly but happily facing east or west.

Most roses find the honeysuckle a little too overwhelming as a climbing companion and it is true that it can ramble and twine to excess if not controlled.

In warm parts of the country and in sheltered positions in a well-drained soil the passion flower

---

This rambler rose has had its pendulous shoots tied to an umbrella-shaped wire framework

A rambler rose, the deep pink Minnehaha, trained on a tripod, an effective method of display

(*Passiflora caerulea*) will bear its distinguished flower and egg-shaped fruit. Its fascinating tendrils cling tight but kindly and the intriguing ivory-white variety Constance Elliott is always worth a trial.

For the adventurous prepared to grow a climber for its remarkable foliage rather than for its unimportant flower, there is *Actinidia kolomikta*. The leaves are tri-coloured, pink, white and green. Again, provided you have an east to west position and a warm garden you will find *A. kolomikta* an arresting eye-catcher.

Climbing Sports

There are upright climbers, full-petalled and similar to the hybrid tea, single, semi-double and double, all of which are suitable for growing on pillars and walls.

Many of these are climbing sports from dwarf or bush varieties that are completely true to the type, such as Climbing Lady Sylvia. On occasion, the climber is more vigorous than its bush counterpart, as in the case of Climbing Mrs Sam McGredy and Climbing Ena Harkness, both capable of giving exhibition blooms of superb quality.

Climbers other than the perpetuals growing to 10 to 12 feet and having but one flowering period should not be expected to supply as many blooms as bushes of the variety although a good climber in full flush can, from time to time, give a unique performance of 300 blooms.

Some, but by no means all the climbing sports are repeat or recurrent flowerers giving a second performance in the autumn.

There is an unfortunate variation in the many different strains of climbing sports available and it is therefore important that roses should be bought from a reliable source. Poor strains are a menace and should be burned straightaway.

Many rosarians leave their climbers unpruned the first year unless they are over-exuberant for fear of their reverting to their dwarf form.

As the climbers mature they develop the habit of flowering at their extremities, and side shoots should be induced to grow at an angle or better still horizontally to encourage flowering. This training must be done when the wood is young and sufficiently supple to allow itself to be bent into place. When the old stems lose their vitality they must be cut back to lively wood or be removed altogether.

The climbing sports can be trained to cover fences and will travel about half the length horizontally that they would have reached if growing upright. Meanwhile, it is not always remembered that the rose is effective in covering any ugly object in the garden and is a fast mover even if a little slow in establishing itself.

The climbing sports do not require a steeplejack to prune them for few reach more than 15 feet.

CLIMBING SPORTS OF HYBRID TEAS

CLIMBING ENA HARKNESS: splendid crimson-scarlet red that gives magnificent well-formed blooms if grown horizontally. Beautifully fragrant. Height, 10 to 12 feet.

CLIMBING ETOILE DE HOLLANDE: rich red. Gives a repeat performance in the autumn. Fruity scent; a rampant grower. Height, 15 feet.

Rosa filipes *Kiftsgate growing on an apple tree in Mrs. Margery Fish's garden at East Lambrook Manor, South Petherton, Somerset* (see p. 93)

CLIMBING LADY HILLINGDON: rich apricot-yellow; perpetual flowerer seen at its best as a climber. If carefully trained will climb to the roof.

CLIMBING MADAME CAROLINE TESTOUT: clear pale pink; perhaps the most rewarding of the climbing sports; flowers again in September. The tallest of the group which will, when left to itself, grow to the bedroom windows; an old rose that has retained its vigour and air of romance.

CLIMBING MADAME EDOUARD HERRIOT: orange-salmon. Spectacular in June; some bloom in the autumn. Height, 12 feet.

CLIMBING MRS SAM MCGREDY: one of the best with an explosion of sunset shaded blooms. Once established repeat flowering. Height 15 to 18 feet.

CLIMBING OPHELIA: flesh-pink, sweetly scented and repeat flowering. Height, 10 feet.

CLIMBING SHOT SILK: rose and gold; flowers again in September. Height, 8 to 10 feet.

CLIMBING SPEK'S YELLOW: deep yellow; rather half-hearted repeat-bloom in the autumn. Height, 10 feet.

Note: Climbing Peace is not recommended being a shy flowerer in this country.

Meg, a coral-salmon, golden centred climber (see p. 88)

The richly-scented Madame Gregoire Staechelin

Climbing Roses of the Hybrid Tea Type

These vigorous climbers need plenty of room and scope. They may be pruned severely, as being true climbers there is no tendency to revert to dwarf form.

GLOIRE DE DIJON (Noisettiana variety): buff-yellow, large and double with a tinge of rose. Some strains have unfortunately deteriorated but fine old specimens do exist. Height, 12 to 15 feet.

GUINÉE: dark red with black maroon shading of velvet quality. One of the most perpetual of the climbing roses. Small heavily scented flowers carried singly and in clusters. Height 8 to 10 feet.

LAWRENCE JOHNSTON: hybrid Pernetiana variety originally known as Hidcote Yellow. Loosely formed semi-double, canary-yellow blooms with fragrance. Height, 25 feet.

MADAME ALFRED CARRIÈRE (Noisettiana variety): one of the finest white climbers. Hardy, free-flowering throughout the summer and very fragrant. Suitable for a northern aspect, that will cover a large area of house-wall. Height, 25 feet.

MADAME GREGOIRE STAECHELIN: glorious climber, carmine in bud, developing into a superb pink with splashes of carmine on the outside of the petals. Richly scented, this rose flowers at the end of June and into July. Height, 15 feet.

PAUL'S LEMON PILLAR: pale lemon-yellow to white, large, full and fragrant. Summer flowering only. Height, 10 to 12 feet.

Right: *Climbing Madame Caroline Testout on an outbuilding*

Perpetual-flowering Climbers

This group, suitable for walls and pillars, is much in demand because of its abundance of bloom. Due to their free-flowering habit, growth is restricted and easily controlled.

In this group must be included the glorious Wilhelm Kordes introductions. Single red Dortmund with a white eye is a Kordesii variety that should not be missed. The Kordesii group in the main grow to some 6 feet and are particularly useful for screens or pillars.

DANSE DU FEU: orange-red, double flowers blooming throughout the season into November. An excellent pillar rose. Height, 7 to 8 feet.

GOLDEN SHOWERS: golden-yellow, semi-double blooms. Flowers freely at intervals. Height, 7 to 8 feet. Colour illustration on pp. 90-91.

HAMBURGER PHOENIX: a Kordesii introduction. Rich scarlet-crimson, semi-double, scented perpetual with decorative hips. Height, 8 to 10 feet.

MEG: short climber suited to pillars. Large clusters of semi-double, coral-salmon blooms with golden centres. An enchanting rose. Height, 10 feet.

MERMAID: single 5 inch-wide cream bloom with striking golden stamens. A continuous flowerer from July until the frosts arrive. Almost evergreen in mild parts of the country. Can also be grown as a large specimen bush. One of the best climbers we have. Height, 20 to 30 feet.

NEW DAWN: this shell-pink rose bears delicately scented flowers in profusion throughout the summer. Height, 10 to 12 feet. Colour illustration on p. 90.

PINK PERPETUE (introduced 1965): it is regrettable that this lovely rose has not been given a truly French or English name for it is a beauty. The buds are carmine opening to clear rose. Height, 15 feet. Colour illustration on p. 90.

ZÉPHIRINE DROUHIN: a Bourbon variety introduced in 1868 that has made a comeback. Rosy-cerise. Strong, hardy and thornless, it has a raspberry scent. Height, 15 feet.

The free-flowering Kordesii roses—particularly useful for screens or pillars

Mermaid

Left: *Alberic Barbier, with yellow buds opening to creamy-white, is a useful climber for screening*

Below: *A gateway surrounded by roses makes an elegant frame for the view beyond*

Ramblers

Ramblers, mostly wichuraianas, are primarily used for pergolas, arches and pillars, but look extremely well sprawling over sloping banks, rockeries or tree trunks, or tumbling over a wall. They will make as much progress lengthwise hugging the ground as they would have climbing upright.

Alas, they give but one splendid display after which the dead-heads should be immediately removed for they are sad and disfiguring.

ALBERIC BARBIER (Wichuraiana hybrid): yellow buds opening a rich creamy-white and slightly scented. Dense shiny foliage – a useful climber for screening. Height, 20 feet.

Below: *New Dawn, a splendid climber with a long flowering season* (see p. 88)

Above: *Pink Perpetue, a climber of outstanding beauty which reaches a height of 15 feet* (see p. 88)

Left: *Golden Showers, a climber which flowers freely at intervals and reaches a height of 7 to 8 feet (see p. 88)*

Above: *The popular rambler Albertine (see p. 92). This variety, which flowers profusely, is shown on a house wall on p. 83*

ALBERTINE (Wichuraiana hybrid): dark copper buds opening salmon-pink with paler edges. A profuse flowerer. Height, 15 to 20 feet. Colour illustration on p. 91.

AMERICAN PILLAR: a single pink rambler with a white centre. A fast-growing, tough variety that needs plenty of space. Useful for covering an eyesore. Height, 15 feet.

CHAPLIN'S PINK CLIMBER: a climber with large warm pink flowers with golden stamens. Sturdy and willing to grow in unpromising cold places. Height, 15 feet.

DOROTHY PERKINS (a Wichuraiana hybrid): brilliant rose-pink. An old timer that has made a half-hearted comeback. Height, 18 feet.

DR W. VAN FLEET (a Wichuraiana hybrid): a lovely blush-pink flower; vigorous and scented. Height, 15 feet.

EMILY GRAY: coppery-yellow rambler with shiny foliage. Early but by no means profuse. Almost evergreen in mild districts. Height, 15 feet.

GOLDFINCH (a Multiflora variety): a lovely soft yellow flowerer semi-double and scented. Much loved by the great gardener Vita Sackville-West. Height, 12 feet.

PAUL'S SCARLET CLIMBER: rich scarlet flowers in lovely clusters, strong and showy. Height, 15 feet.

WEDDING DAY: a lovely *sino-wilsonii* hybrid with glossy green leaves and yellow buds opening white. The petals are unusual being pointed, stained with pink as they fade. Must be watched for mildew. Possesses a sweet orange scent. Height, 20 feet.

Dorothy Perkins

Paul's Scarlet Climber

Species and Hybrids

There are a number of wild species and similar varieties, both old and new, that will climb or scramble to considerable heights. I remember seeing *R. moyesii* reaching up high among the trees in a lovely garden in Richmond, Yorkshire, seemingly as happy as in its native home in the highlands of Asia. Many such as *R. filipes* are too large and boisterous for small gardens, but given space they are effective and extremely sweet-scented.

R. BANKSIAE LUTEA: Chinese rambler. Delightful small bunches of butter-yellow pompons that arrive in May. Slightly tender, requiring a sheltered position and a warm wall when it will grow to 40 feet.

Rosa filipes *Kiftsgate (see also illustration on p. 85).*

CLIMBING CÉCILE BRUNNER: hybrid China floribunda with flesh pink miniature flowers of exquisite shape. Also known as Sweetheart rose. Height, 20 feet.

FÉLICITÉ ET PERPÉTUE (a sport of *R. sempervirens*): the Queen of white ramblers, many-petalled and delicately scented, opening from round, ruby-shaded buds. Still seen decorating many cottages in the remoter parts of the country. Very hardy, mid-season flowerer. Height, 12 feet.

R. FILIPES KIFTSGATE: *R. filipes* comes from western China but Kiftsgate was found in a Gloucestershire garden. The rose is smothered in small creamy, deliciously scented flowers about 1½ inches across, with orange-yellow stamens. A giant climber that needs a large garden where it can sprawl. Height and spread both 30 feet.

FORTUNE'S YELLOW (*R. banksiae* hybrid): deep straw-yellow with flush of rich carmine. Worth cosseting in a warm garden on a warm wall. Height, 18 feet.

R. MOSCHATA (the musk rose): wild and vigorous demanding a large wall facing south or west or space where it can climb into a tree. Small white flowers of lovely fragrance followed by small red heps. Height, 60 feet.

R. LAEVIGATA ANEMONE (syn. *R. sinica* Anemone): an exquisite hybrid; a single silvery pink with deeper veining. Height, 15 feet.

RAMONA (a *R. laevigata* [syn. *R. sinica*] sport). an enormous single carmine-pink flower, silver backed with golden stamens. Fragrant and resplendent in the early summer. Height, 15 feet.

Rosa filipes, *an especially vigorous white-flowered rambler from western China*

Polyantha or Poly-Pompons

The history of the Poly-Pompons opened in 1860 when the seed of *R. multiflora* was imported from Japan, but it was not until 1909 that the important variety Orleans Rose made its appearance.

The Edwardians planted the dwarf polyantha as freely as the rosarians plant the floribunda today. The characteristics of the group were distinct: they were hardy, between 15 and 18 inches high, compact and bushy and the semi-single or double button flowers an inch in diameter, coming in cluster-rambler formation.

Orleans Rose was responsible for a number of sports, flowering freely from early summer to late autumn, taking short rests between the bursts and even flowering on until Christmas in mild districts. The secondary shoot below the flower head takes over when a flush has faded and the small bush bursts into bloom once again.

The polyantha is to be had in gay colours and perhaps looks its best in a sunny border away from its modern and larger brothers. The success of the floribundas has checked the popularity of the dwarfs but has by no means ousted them and there should be a special place in the garden for the best varieties.

Unfortunately, the group is prone to mildew and alas carries little if any scent.

Poly-Pompons

BABY FAURAX: lavender-purple. Height, 1 foot.

CAMEO: salmon. Height, 2 feet.

ÉBLOUISSANT: deep clear red, large flowers with rather ragged petals. Height, 1½ feet.

ELLEN POULSEN: pink. Height, 2 feet.

GLOIRE DU MIDI: geranium scarlet introduced by de Ruiter, 1932. Some rosarians give this dwarf the credit for bringing the brilliant pelargonium orange-scarlet pigment into the rose family. Height, 2 feet.

GOLDEN SALMON SUPÉRIEURE: bright unfading orange-salmon. Height, 2 feet.

GRUMPY: tawney-red semi-double. Height, 1 foot.

HAPPY: double rich crimson. A cushion plant. Height, 1 foot.

HOLLANDIA: small, double unfading red. Height, 2 feet.

JEAN MERMOZ: deep china pink. Short and profuse, makes a good edging. Height, 1½ feet.

LITTLE WHITE PET: introduced in 1879. A dream of a dwarf that must not be missed. I hesitate to state its height as in strong soils it can grow quite tall. Unfortunately, becoming rather scarce. Height, about 2 feet.

PAUL CRAMPEL: vivid and as showy as the pelargonium with which it shares its name. Height, 2 to 3 feet.

PINKIE: rose-pink. Short and pleasing. Height, 1 foot.

PYGMY RED: rich crimson. Short and free. Height, 1 foot.

THE FAIRY: clusters of clear coral-pink and a dwarf sport of Lady Godiva. Has a spreading bushy growth. Height, depending on soil, about 1½ feet.

YVONNE RABIER: white, tall and slightly scented. Height, 3 feet.

Note: Cécile Brunner, also known as the Sweetheart rose, should also be remembered as a dwarf. This gem of a miniature has flesh-pink flowers of exquisite shape. Height, 1½ feet. It is usually listed as a China or Old Rose, introduced 1880.

Miniature Roses

These are true miniature bushes of 4 to 12 inches in height, and in perfect proportion with their large counterparts. Grown by specialists from cuttings, they keep their miniature habit.

Being completely hardy they are suited for rock gardens or the front of the border. They do not survive long indoors or in any window-box, trough or container unless it is well-drained and at least 18 inches deep.

There is a place for these tiny plants in the garden, possibly in a pocket in the stonework or an old wall or building. Planted in the herbaceous border with phlox and poppies as neighbours they are quick to disappear.

A formal table garden of dwarf miniature roses only is always a great attraction at the Chelsea Flower Show.

The dwarfs should be planted 9 or 12 inches apart and require trimming rather than pruning. It must also be remembered when choosing a position for them that they enjoy the sun. Strong shoots may appear and should be cut back half way and it is important that the flowers should be removed as they fade.

R. chinensis minima made its appearance in 1805 and was followed by a number of variations, among them *R. roulettii,* still one of the best of the group and only 6 inches high when grown on its own roots. All varieties grow taller when budded on briar and for this reason it is better to buy from a miniature specialist who grows from cuttings. Some nurserymen prefer to graft rather than to bud.

BABY GOLD: the deepest of the yellows. Height, 12 to 15 inches.

BABY MASQUERADE: flame and gold – immensely popular. Height, 10 to 15 inches.

HUMPTY DUMPTY: bright rose-pink, very short. Height, 4 to 6 inches.

JUNE TIME: double light pink – pretty. Height, 9 to 12 inches.

MIDGET: carmine to crimson; white at base. Height, 6 inches.

NEW PENNY: salmon. Height, 9 inches.

PERLA DE MONTSERRAT: rose-pink, a miniature Lady Sylvia. Height, 12 to 15 inches.

PIXIE ROSE: deep pink, double. Height, 9 inches.

POUR TOI: white with a hint of green at its base. Height, 12 inches.

PRINCE CHARMING: scarlet-crimson. Height, 8 to 12 inches.

ROULETTII: rose-pink, a veteran. Height, 9 to 12 inches.

SCARLET GEM: double scarlet. Height, 9 to 12 inches.

SWEET FAIRY: rose. Scented. Height, 8 to 10 inches.

TOMMY TUCKER: pink; a charmer. Height, 6 inches.

WILLIE WINKIE: double pink; very free-flowering. Height, 6 to 10 inches.

YELLOW BANTAM: light sulphur yellow; the smallest of them all. Height, 3 to 4 inches.

Climbing Miniatures

CLIMBING JACKIE: the only climbing yellow.

CLIMBING MAGIC WAND: bright red with a white eye.

CLIMBING PINK CAMEO: bright pink, a perpetual flowerer and the best of the miniature climbers. Weeping standards on 15-inch stems are sometimes available.

CLIMBING POMPON DE PARIS: rose with exquisite foliage that will reach 5 to 6 feet.

SHOWOFF: buff with touches of red and orange. Semi-single.

Miniature standard roses and miniature weeping standards are to be had of many of the varieties mentioned on 12- to 18-inch stems.

Roses Under Glass

A rose out of season, in the frost, rain or snow, is a delight and roses in May very much a luxury. I doubt that many gardeners with an empty un-heated greenhouse are aware that roses can be grown in an unheated greenhouse. I have learnt from my mail that many novice gardeners who inherit a greenhouse are often bedevilled as to what to grow. I hope this chapter will give them a lead. The May-flowering rose is as easy and certainly more glamorous than the cineraria, lachenalia or pelargonium.

If blooms are wanted earlier than May, then the amateur will find that electricity is the most practical way of providing the heat. A strip electric heater wire installed, I suggest, by a professional, will provide roses in April. The thermostat should be watched with an eagle eye otherwise there may be blind shoots and cracked pots. An oil emergency heater should be kept handy to avoid a crisis should the electricity be cut during a severe late freeze once the roses have started growth.

A temperature kept within the range of 45° to 50°F. is ideal from October to April. To obtain this should the temperature fall low at night a boost of some 20° to 30° is required. But much will depend on the size of the house, its position and the climate.

Roses for Christmas are a luxury best left to the trained and professional. The forcing necessary will greatly increase the expense. Meanwhile, the varieties grown must be chosen with care as few roses thrive in high temperatures.

Planting

Roses can be grown in pots, or better still, if the greenhouse is to be given up to them, they can be planted directly in the soil. Not only must the top 12 inches of the soil be turned over, but the lower sub-soil must be broken down and fresh compost introduced.

This must be of high quality such as top spit grassland that has had time to rot down, with a generous amount of granulated peat to hold the moisture, plus 6 ounces of hoof and horn and 6 ounces of ground bone, or John Innes Base Fertiliser as directed. It is important that the peat should be well soaked before it is used.

The compost should be well mixed before being introduced into the bed or pots in September and then copiously watered ready for planting in October. This mixture will keep the plants well nourished for the first year but further feeding with fertiliser will be needed annually.

Roses should always be planted firmly, allowing 15 inches between the plants and at least 1½ feet between the rows: the closer the planting the harder will be the pruning required. Because of the limited space the January pruning has to be more severe in the greenhouse than outdoors.

The roses should not be started into growth before February, when watering should begin in earnest, saturating the soil. After watering feeding can begin with a reputable fertiliser containing superphosphate and potash. This should be first hoed then watered in.

From now onwards good ventilation is all-important, otherwise sweating followed by a dangerous form of mildew are likely to develop. Top ventilation available in a large greenhouse is a great advantage. The gardener with a small greenhouse with side ventilators must use those facing west rather than east, keep the door shut, and avoid draughts as best he can.

The gardener buying a new greenhouse should on no account economise on ventilators. Two at the top and one on each side lower down are needed if the greenhouse is of any size. Perhaps I should add that extra ventilation entails extra watering and damping down.

Syringe in the morning. Spraying against mildew is safer under glass than dusting with green sulphur. Water regularly, tapping the pots with a wooden mallet while listening for the hollow ring that denotes dryness. Fumigate with nicotine against greenfly and thrips and provide azobenzene against red spider if this is troublesome. Provide moveable sunlight blinds or, alternatively, sprinkle the glass with whitewash to filter the sunshine.

The plants will flower 12 to 14 weeks after bringing them inside and happily they will last longer than blooms grown outdoors. Only one flower should be allowed to a branch, and the grower is asked to satisfy himself with no more than six roses on a plant.

Once flowering is over at the end of May, the pots can be placed outside for the summer. A piece of perforated zinc put over the drainage hole will defeat the intrusion of worms.

A second crop of flowers will arrive in June and July and the gardener should resist cutting these with long stalks and so give the plants the opportunity of building up food reserves.

In September it may be necessary to promote the strong and vigorous to larger 8- or 9-inch pots, and having scraped away the tired soil, the plants will need top-dressing with fresh compost.

The Plants

Plants may be lifted from the garden for indoor growing but if they are to be bought the gardener is advised to visit the local nursery and pick out plants with a few strong well-ripened shoots that will respond far better than those with a mass of inferior growth.

Many rosarians prefer to pot up rooted cuttings of *R. rugosa* and do their own budding, but I would not advise this course for the beginner.

Varieties

When it comes to choosing varieties much will depend on the colour, the quantity of blooms and the quality wished for.

Lady Sylvia has a reputation second to none for doing well under glass and her light pink, yellow based, pointed blooms are seen in every florist's shop throughout the winter season. She has few dangerous thorns and has the added advantage of scent. But some gardeners will wish to grow the less familiar – perhaps the warm pink Gavotte; cream tipped and flushed crimson, suffused yellow Perfecta or scarlet-red Karl Herbst. I personally do not tire of the scarlet Ena Harkness – at its best the perfect rose.

Full-flowered varieties with 28 or more petals are the best sorts for the greenhouse. Yellow roses are inclined to be temperamental. However, I saw Dr. A. J. Verhage grown to perfection at Chelsea last year and have heard a good report of King's Ransom. Deep vermillion Baccara deserves a special word because of the splendid way it lasts as a cut flower.

Floribundas are less obliging under glass than the hybrid teas but pure white Iceberg with its pink tinged buds sometimes proves itself an exception to the rule.

The unblemished rose grown under glass excels all those grown outdoors and has a beauty that astonishes like a baby asleep.

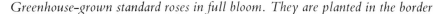

Greenhouse-grown standard roses in full bloom. They are planted in the border

Exhibiting

Exhibiting is the greatest fun for all but the unhappy cup hunters. The successful exhibitor is usually a highly knowledgable gardener who has given months of care and undivided attention to his plants to reach the high standard demanded. There are no short cuts and the 'most perfect phase of their beauty' asked for in the schedule is learnt from the gardener's own mistakes and other people's successes.

By experience only will the gardener learn how to hurry slow-coach Frau Karl Druschki that often takes as long as 14 weeks to bring into flower after pruning; or to hold back fast-moving Perfecta that bursts into bloom in little more than 10 weeks after the use of the knife, so that both these varieties may take their place in the exhibition box on the appointed day at the end of June or the beginning of July.

Special feeding with a well-balanced soluble fertiliser, as directed, when the soil is damp is an important part of the exhibitor's routine. After the summer show feeding should be withheld unless the roses need a boost in July for the autumn show. There is always a danger of encouraging lush, sappy growth that has not the time to ripen before the frosts arrive, and the exhibitor depends on well-ripened wood of the previous year for his winning blooms.

Special Classes

Every encouragement is given to the novice showman, and there are not only special classes for him, but also different classes for the owners of big gardens and small, for those who only grow 50, 100 or 250 as well as the amateur who can pick from his thousands.

Ideally, the beginner should start showing locally where he will get the practical experience he needs. Each variety of rose is judged on its merits so that the good small rose has its chance against such varieties as Pink Favourite and other whoppers.

Top: *Karl Herbst, deep red with paler reverse, is a fine exhibition rose*

Above: *Perfecta, which has light rose-pink flowers shading paler, is a superb exhibition variety*

98

Left: *An exhibition arrangement of the variety Dr A. J. Verhage*

Below: *Potential exhibition blooms covered with waterproof protectors to avoid damage by sun and rain*

Bottom: *The variety Peace, arranged by Sheila Macqueen*

Points and Faults

The judge looks for form and shape, freshness, erectness, brilliance, purity of colour, long stems and clean, shining foliage. As already pointed out, size is not stressed by the pundits but the old saying holds good – 'a good big'un will always beat a good little'un.'

Among the more serious defects to be avoided by the exhibitor are showing blooms with split centres; damaged, marked or faded petals; coarseness and over-dressing.

Less than one per cent of rose growers are exhibitors, and those among the other 99 per cent who do not recognise a split centre when they see one will enjoy lovely Rose Gaujard in spite of her shortcomings. But the showman will condemn a rose that fails in its formation whatever its charm, and if he has his way will chase it out of the catalogues.

By kind permission of the Royal National Rose Society, I give their Audit Table that includes only varieties introduced into this country before January, 1963.

First twelve exhibition varieties for northern counties:

Peace	Super Star
Wendy Cussons	Gail Borden
Perfecta	Brilliant
Stella	Royal Highness
Pink Favourite	Isabel de Ortiz
Memoriam	Rose Gaujard

First twelve exhibition varieties for southern counties:

Pink Favourite	Isabel de Ortiz
Perfecta	Peace
Wendy Cussons	Brilliant
Memoriam	Super Star
Stella	Anne Letts
Royal Highness	Silver Lining

Disbudding

Side buds should be removed from the hybrid teas so that the central bud may develop. They snap off quite easily but care must be taken not to damage the central bud in any way.

Floribundas do not require disbudding but on occasions the truss benefits if the centre flower – that is the first to bloom – is removed, so that the remainder of the flowers give a more uniform performance.

If a main bud clearly looks as if it will be ahead of the show date, there is an excuse for leaving a side bud that will flower later as a standby.

Bloom Protection

During the last exciting few weeks before the show hybrid tea blooms must be given protection against sun and rain. Such blooms as Perfecta generally need covering with waterproof protectors, these being clipped to bamboo sticks and so positioned that the rim of the protector comfortably covers the bloom without preventing the free circulation of air.

I remember once visiting Mr F. A. Gibson, a past President of the Royal National Rose Society, just before the Southport Flower Show and finding his rose garden a mass of protectors resembling a miniature site of campers' tents. But how thrilling it was to peep under the rim of a protector and see a potential prize winner.

Tying

Three or four days before the show the blooms must be tied in with the softest of knitting-wool. The outside rows of petals should be opened out so that they almost lie flat and the next row be allowed to fill the space between these and the cone. When dealing with a many-petalled rose, it may be wiser to open out three rows of petals rather than two.

Having cut the wool into lengths, it should be passed round the cone when dry, and the tie made tight enough to hold the petals together and check them from opening before the show.

Once the flowers have opened, it is too late to think about tying.

Cutting

If the show is within, say, 50 miles of the garden, then cutting can be delayed until the early morning of the show; but for greater distances this is impracticable and cutting is best done in the late afternoon of the day before the show. Where really long distances are involved, possibly as much as 50 hours will elapse between the time of cutting and judging.

Specimen blooms can be cut with short stems as they are exhibited in the regulation boxes but blooms to be arranged in vases for exhibiting in other classes must be long stemmed. Once cut they should be plunged to their necks in buckets of deep water and the stems not allowed to dry out again before the show. Much is to be gained by observation and the beginner would do well to watch, for instance, the swiftness with which Picture opens in comparison with the more dilatory Super Star.

An immaculate display of blooms in an exhibition box

A box to hold six exhibition roses

The bucket should be put in some cool place for the night, if the show is not until the following day. It is the long night's drink that gives the blooms the stamina to stand up to the stresses of show day.

The showman is advised to remove the lower thorns on the stem but not to smash or pulp the stalks as is the practice of some florists and flower arrangers. This is more harmful than helpful.

When it comes to cutting, practical experience is invaluable; the veteran showman who knows each variety and the pace at which it opens, has the pull.

Exhibition Boxes

The classes for blooms displayed in exhibition boxes, each box containing 6, 12 or more individual blooms, are usually the highlight of the show, the blooms displayed representing an exalted standard of cultivation.

The base of the box should be covered with a layer of fresh green moss as an attractive background. The short stems should then be placed so that their base reaches the bottom of the water tubes with the calyx resting on the cross piece at the top of the wire support that is to be found at the back of each water-tube. The stem can then be wired to this stiff support.

The best bloom should be given pride of place at the top left-hand corner and be divorced from the smaller fry: a good general effect should be the aim. Roses being entered in exhibition box classes are best taken to the show in their boxes but long-stemmed blooms for display in vases require transporting in water-filled buckets.

Packing and Transport

Whenever possible, the roses should be packed in tins or buckets which allow them to take up water while in transit, and they should be covered with loose polythene bags to keep them fresh. The blooms should also be fairly tightly packed together to prevent shaking.

During recent years, *Lonicera nitida,* the popular evergreen hedging plant, has been widely used not only for packing roses, but also to give weak stalks support in the vases. Although wiring is allowed, and stub-wires are useful for holding roses in

Dressing a show bloom with a camel-hair brush

An exhibition bowl of roses

position in a vase and supporting the weak-necked, it must be skilfully placed for judges have eagle eyes (they are allowed to peer round corners but not to touch!). Ties can be removed to see that they are not causing damage to the petals but they must then be replaced until just before judging starts. Blotting paper will be found a blessing for absorbing moisture on petals after a storm or some misadventure during transit.

Dressing

The showman must, of course, make the most of his blooms and camouflage any defective petals as best he can without over-dressing. But he must have a care in this for the judges demote the unnaturally bent or manipulated bloom that bears the mark, if not the finger-print, of man and is not in accordance with the characteristics of the variety.

Whereas the amateur generally uses a broad camel-hair brush for dressing his blooms, the nurseryman makes do with finger and thumb and reflexes a petal to disguise a minor blemish on an adjacent petal as if by magic.

Vases

Staging roses in vases demands more skill than staging in exhibition boxes. The simplest and, therefore, usually the best method is to place the two longest stemmed blooms at the back of the vase, three in the middle row and a short-stemmed sturdy bloom alone in the front. A vase of three specimen blooms seems to fall naturally into an inverted triangle; in the single specimen bloom class only full petalled blooms should be expected to face the competition. Floribundas, ramblers, climbers, shrub and cluster roses of all types should bear trusses of maximum size flowers of uniform development.

In these decorative classes the fresh, the brilliant and the shapely win points. Floribundas should contribute a mass of bloom but it may take as many as ten stems to make a telling bowl, which entails growing a considerable number of plants.

Unhurried Preparation

Allow yourself plenty of time to find your allotted position and class card, and do not hurry the placing of labels and the arranging and untying of the blooms. Avoid getting upset if one of the thinner roses flies open and shatters almost as soon as the tie is undone. These things do happen and it might be wise to make a note not to show the offending variety again. Meanwhile, one of the spares which must always be on hand for such emergencies can be used to fill the gap.

Finally have a last look round to see that everything conforms with the schedule. Tilt the base of the box at the back with a wedge or small flower pot and lift the back row of water-tubes in their sockets to the desired height. Then arrange the vases in the second row similarly to leave them in a slightly lower position. Then turn the class card face downwards, and keeping your fingers crossed, go and have a nice cool drink!

Part Three

Hedges
Making a Standard Rose
Weeping Standards
Ground Cover
Roses in Containers
Fragrance
Pot-pourri

Hedges

How wonderful it would be if by some miracle half the miserable privet hedges in this country disappeared and were replaced by hedges of roses. True the rose barrier might be a trifle thin during the winter months but so indeed are the miserable privets – so what of it? The summer parade would be a glorious affair and generous recompense for any winter shortcomings.

Top left: Canary Bird, a beautiful rose with bright yellow flowers, as the name implies;
top right: Rosa californica plena, a semi-double pink variety with fern-like foliage;
bottom left: Frühlingsmorgen, a pink-flowered variety, yellow at the base of the petals;
bottom right: The Bourbon variety Madame Ernst Calvat, with pink, fragrant flowers

Boundary and Field Hedges

Sweet briar (*R. rubiginosa*) will defeat both cattle and boys. Its flowering season is short but the scent of its foliage on a hot day after a shower is delicious and the plant acts as a willing host to both wild and cultivated clematis.

Sweet briar planted $2\frac{1}{2}$–3 feet apart or *R. multiflora japonica* planted a little closer should make a fairly cheap impenetrable boundary hedge up to 7 to 8 feet tall.

The Penzance briars are more showy and robust and carry heps in the autumn, but, unfortunately, like all the briars, they are vulnerable both to mildew and black spot. They have a similar habit to the wild rose and call for discipline. The Austrian Briars are sparse growers and seldom form a stout boundary hedge.

Shrub and Old-Fashioned Roses

There are a number of wild roses and their close relations that make effective screens or hedges. One of the most beautiful is Canary Bird, a spring-flowering rose from Korea, probably related to *R. xanthina spontanea*. It grows 5 to 6 feet tall. However, a warning should be given – this charmer does not grow willingly on all soils and the gardener is fortunate if it settles down in his domain.

Other shrub roses that can be trained as screens are the 5 foot tall *R. californica plena*, a semi-double, pink variety with fern-like foliage; *R. complicata*, a variety whose single pink flowers with a white eye are carried on graceful stems; or one of the *spinosissima* hybrids belonging to the Frühlings group raised by Wilhelm Kordes. The soft cream-yellow Frühlingsgold with deep yellow stamens makes a heavenly screen of about 8 feet, as does the 6 foot Frühlingsmorgen with single pink flowers that merge into yellow at their base. The ivory-white Frühlingsanfang, growing to 6 or 7 feet, is not only beautiful but scented and should not be missed.

On occasions, when a squat hedge is wanted within a garden on either side of a path or to form a dividing line between one part of the garden and another, the single, pink *R. nitida* will fill the bill.

Many of the old-fashioned roses can be used for fences, and in one garden I know of, a carefully-trained screen of the cerise-magenta Tour de Malakoff, a *centifolia* variety, accompanied by the cerise-crimson *gallica* velvety Charles de Mills succeed in masking, at least during the summer, a neighbour's hideous garage, while the *alba* roses Maiden's Blush and Céleste (Celestial), and a moss rose whose name I cannot recall, manage to camouflage an equally ugly summerhouse.

The sturdier Bourbon roses can be readily trained to strong wooden or wire supports stretched between poles or pillars. Zéphirine Drouhin with its charm and its more or less perpetual-flowering habit makes one of the most beautiful screens imaginable. I can also recommend pink Madame Ernst Calvat; Madame Isaac Pereire, light madder crimson and one of the great roses of the 19th century; and flat, soft, creamy-blush Souvenir de la Malmaison, a real climber that only needs a helping hand to climb to 10 feet.

The China rose Old Blush, with semi-double pink flowers which can sometimes be seen in bloom in Christmas week, has something special about it if only as a buttonhole rose. It will grow to 7 or 8 feet and is perpetual-flowering. I can also recommend another rose of this type for hedging purposes – the crimson Gruss an Teplitz.

The hybrid musks are repeat-flowering, sturdy and self-supporting and can be trained as screens to over 5 feet.

A fine hedge of the hybrid musk rose Penelope, with fragrant, creamy salmon-pink flowers

The creamy salmon-pink Penelope is the favourite member of the group but the copper-apricot Cornelia is excellent for cutting. Felicia in two tones of silver-pink is a splendid hedge-maker and I notice that Buff Beauty is favoured by Regent's Park. The hybrid musks are, as a rule, scented.

Planted 4 feet apart, they require only light pruning but should be regularly tied in. They enjoy light soil and sunshine.

The Rugosas are, without doubt, the best of the

shrub roses for hedges. Provided they are well cared for they will keep out man and beast.

The musk hedge should always be cut back sufficiently to keep the base of the plants well furnished with foliage. Some rosarians clip the rugosas back ruthlessly to encourage flowering.

The flowers have a lovely clove fragrance and bloom from May to October. The flowers of the single rugosas are followed by fuchsia-pink heps of distinguished shape. This group is particularly blessed in that it is free from pests.

I have many favourites among these perpetual flowerers. Blanc Double de Coubert, papery-white, 6 feet tall; the crimson-purple Roseraie de l'Haÿ (7 feet) and the silver-pink Conrad Ferdinand Meyer (8 feet) are high on my list. But I am always glad to see charming pink F. J. Grootendorst; the semi-double, mallow pink Sarah van Fleet, with cream stamens, that makes a superb hedge some 6 feet tall, and beloved 5-foot-tall, double-white Schneezwerg, the 'Snow Dwarf.' In addition, the red Scabrosa makes one of the finest dense hedges of 4 to 5 feet.

Ramblers and Climbers

These make attractive screens or informal hedges given the necessary support, and are dealt with on pp. 80 to 93. Creamy-yellow Mermaid growing to 25 ft. is a shining star.

Modern Hybrid Shrub Roses

The modern cross-bred hybrids are difficult to place under any particular heading. Many of them are perpetual-flowering and some of them of superb quality and suitable for hedges or screens.

Nevada, reputed to be a descendant of *R. moyesii,* is the outstanding member of this group. It is the largest of the shrub roses and being a dense grower needs plenty of space. The arching branches are decked with lovely single white blooms and a mature specimen of 7 or 8 feet in height in flower in late May or June is a superb sight. The second burst of flowering is a good deal inferior to the first. It is a feast for the eye but, alas, without scent.

Zéphirine Drouhin, a Bourbon variety with rosy-cerise flowers, is a magnificent rose for screening purposes

Below: *The pink Rugosa variety F. J. Grootendorst*

The shrub rose Nevada, an arresting sight in the full flush of its flowering

The shrub rose Frühlingsgold, which makes a colourful screen

Floribundas

Queen Elizabeth, Frensham and other giant floribundas are sometimes listed as shrub roses growing, as they do, to 5 feet. A single row of Queen Elizabeth planted $2\frac{1}{2}$ feet apart, or a double staggered row will make a thick hedge 3 feet wide. The plants should be pruned of some outside growth to check their tendency to legginess. The scarlet-crimson Frensham appears to have lost resistance to mildew in most parts of the country and is an ill-advised choice. Dorothy Wheatcroft, Evelyn Fison, Gustav Frahm and Scarlet Queen Elizabeth are reds to take its place.

Iceberg, white and vigorous, is also eminently suitable for forming a decorative hedge, or the adventurous might prefer the shorter magenta-rose with an Edwardian look, Escapade.

I now close the subject hoping that, when autumn comes, somewhere a gardener may replace his miserable privet with the rose. I should be happy to hear from him.

Making a Standard Rose

There is a fascination in watching the budded dormant eye develop into the 'head' of a standard rose. It is a short wait, 12 months at most will see it through, and the marriage taking place almost at eye level can be watched closely and in comfort.

The gardener has a choice of a number of rootstocks, among them *canina*, *rugosa* or *multiflora*.

The *canina* rootstock has the advantage in that it appears to have a longer life than the rest and provides grand exhibition roses. It is, however, very prone to suckering. Many growers favour *rugosa* but there are complaints that much of its vigour declines after six or seven years; *multiflora*, as a rootstock, dislikes alkaline soil and cold districts but is fast-growing and makes large trees.

There are certain nurseries that specialise in rootstocks and supplies can be purchased from such establishments, or the gardener can dig a suitable wild rose from the hedgerow with, of course, the permission of the landowner.

Digging out the rose is likely to be a prickly undertaking and requires a good spade, sharp secateurs, leather gloves and old clothes. This work is best done in the autumn when the weather is kind and the earth still warm and favourable for transplanting. Straight-stemmed, two- or three-year-old briars are obviously the ones to look for. All side growths and head growth should be cut from the briar leaving a stem of 4 to 4½ feet.

The planting hole, into which a supporting stake is driven prior to planting, should be prepared beforehand. Have a bucketful of good peat compost containing a sprinkling of bonemeal and hoof and horn waiting alongside so that this can be worked in round the roots as planting takes place. Once the briar has been installed and its stem

Budding a standard rose. The buds are positioned as close as possible to the main stem. Left: *A bud is being tied in; the one on the left awaits tying and the bark has been lifted on the other lateral ready for the insertion of the bud.* Right: *Provided the lower buds 'take' satisfactorily, the top lateral and stem below should be removed later at the white line*

safely secured to a strong stake there is no more to be done until the spring. New shoots will break from the briar stem early in the year when the gardener must decide the height at which the standard is to be grown. (The stem of a full standard is 3 feet 6 inches tall, a half standard 2 to 2½ feet and 'dot' plants 1 to 1½ feet.) Shoots above the desired height should now be removed and limited to four in number.

When the shoots have reached about ¼ inch in thickness at their base (where they join the stem) the ordinary budding procedure (see p. 53) can go forward, the bud being inserted into the upper side of the laterals or side-shoots as close as possible to the main stem. It should be stressed that the closer the bud is to the main stem the more vigorous the head growth will be. When the buds have been positioned and tied in, the young shoots should be given support, otherwise there is a danger that they may be blown out of place by the wind.

Where there are three or four growths it is wise to bud at least two of the shoots, one on each side of the stem, the aim being to give the standard form a nicely balanced 'head.' Should only one bud mature the rose will take longer to develop into a well-shaped 'head.' The usual commercial method is to bud at least three side shoots if well placed.

The buds may swell and break into growth in a week or two or they may lie dormant for many months. Peace and some of the strong-growing varieties are particularly quick movers.

Gardeners are advised to choose varieties of strong constitution and bushy habit for standards are seldom as strong and virile as bushes. A weak 'head' is not worth its keep.

Yellow varieties do not thrive as standards and are often short-lived. Floribundas such as Pink Parfait and Red Dandy are giving a good account of themselves and we are likely to see more standards of this kind of rose.

Budding can be carried out between late June and September. Once the buds are established new growth may be pinched back to encourage sturdiness. Meanwhile, a watch must be kept for suckers at all times; the *rugosa* rootstock is particularly prone to suckering.

The free-flowering floribunda variety Iceberg grown as a standard specimen

An 80-year-old standard of the pale pink hybrid tea Madame Caroline Testout

Weeping Standards

Weeping standards were an Edwardian fashion, and during that period I understand that all leading nurseries held stocks of tall briars budded with wichuraiana ramblers. The best of these were 5½ to 6 feet tall.

These were supported by wire umbrella irons, the main pipe standing close to the stem. Strong support is essential for the weeping standard, particularly in summer when the head is heavy with foliage, and unless fortified and made wind-resistant the stem is likely to be snapped or fractured in the first gale.

Dorothy Perkins and Excelsa were the favourite varieties for this venture, weeping and draping the iron structure without training. But others, the more pliable of the ramblers and wichuraiana group, were trained by canes to droop to their base where a planting of violas in different shades were ready to meet them. The illustrations below show how very effective such roses can be when trained in this way.

When in good heart the canes can be cut out ruthlessly after flowering and new growth be tied in. In this way the performance of the plants can be much improved.

The weepers have now been out of fashion and commerce for three or four decades and are no longer freely available but I notice that several rose specialists have put them once more on offer with stems of 4½ to 5½ feet. Who knows, it may be their turn to be in vogue again? We may live to see Lady Godiva once more 'dotted' on the lawn and here and there Minnehaha weeping in the herbaceous border.

A wichuraiana rose grown as a weeping standard, a form of display which may be due for a return to popularity

The rambler variety Excelsa, rosy-crimson, once a favourite for this kind of display

Ground Cover

The over-worked gardener bedevilled by upkeep problems searches the nurseryman's catalogues for ground-cover plants! *Bergenia cordifolia,* formerly known as *Saxifraga cordifolia;* lamb's ear *(Stachys lanata);* blue bugle *(Ajuga reptans brockbankii);* lady's mantle *(Alchemilla mollis)* and the rest – if you are over-worked and short-handed you may have already turned to these for help. But, strangely enough, although the lamb's ear is never overlooked as a weed smotherer the rose is often disregarded.

However, those who have visited Sissinghurst Castle in Kent will know how useful the hybrid tea Hugh Dickson, can be when pegged down, as taught us by that great gardener Vita Sackville-West. I remember her recommending me to lay down a flat trellis table on my London lawn (which was rather uninteresting) lifting it a little so that clematis and roses planted under it might grow

first through and then in and out of the open-work. A rectangle of rabbit or sheep wire would serve such a purpose equally well. By this method one has the pleasure of looking at the upturned face flower with its lovely expression.

The trailing shoots of Ulrich Brunner, Frau Karl Druschke, Zéphirine Drouhin and Hugh Dickson pegged down by Vita Sackville-West's magic hands broke out from every joint with an exuberant crop of bloom. She rewarded them generously, realising that this method of growing them imposed an extra strain on the roses' stamina and that they therefore needed rich encouragement. With the understanding of a gardener she limited her Hugh Dicksons to four shoots apiece.

The following are a few others fit to join the ground-cover list:

Max Graf, prostrate by nature, will cover a large area without delay. The dense green foliage is decorated with clusters of pink flowers that smell of apples. The hardy short rugosas in white or red provide excellent coverage for banks, but the passer-by must be wary of the thorns. *R. macrantha* is a trailing rose useful for the foreground of a shrubbery or a wasted corner in the wild garden. It has lax branches and delicious, large, single, blush pink blooms. It is a beauty, with fragrance and autumn heps, that enjoys scrambling into trees.

Rosa paulii is another trailer with tough foliage, bearing profuse single white blooms in the spring. There is also a pink version of this procumbent rugosa variety. Both have clove scent. Lastly, there is the rambler Dorothy Perkins that will lie low.

Left: Rugosa and rambler roses and strong-growing bush roses can be pegged down to provide ground cover

Right: The rambler American Pillar grown for ground cover. The stems are tied to a horizontal wire framework

Roses in Containers

The town dweller, short of space and maybe of sun, can make good use of a tub or container. Size is important and a resident rose that is to stay the course must have root-room. Wooden containers are a wise choice for hot, sunny positions as evaporation of moisture is slower in the wooden tub than the earthenware.

There are tubs for all pockets. Wine and beer casks can be converted by the handyman or carpenter. Drainage holes must be provided and the wood treated with Cuprinol and painted with bituminous paint if it is to last.

For those who have more to spend there are the dignified cube Versailles caisses seen outside the large chateaux in France and outside such British houses as Mereworth Castle, Maidstone, Kent. These are usually planted with orange trees but would please the rosarian and satisfy his requirements. They have side panels that slot in and out and in many cases two sides are removed each spring, the exhausted soil being rubbed away to make place for fresh, stimulating fare. Such treatment will enable the plant to prosper and give pleasure indefinitely.

Three delightful tubs and a tank which are perfect fibreglass copies of old lead containers, some dating from the sixteenth century. They are light in weight, strong and frost-proof

Clay Pots

Roses always look well in clay containers and harmonise with other garden features, but the difficulty is to find a size large enough to comfortably house plant-roots. The Vaso range with exciting swag reliefs are decorative and amusing.

Concrete Containers

The low, flat bowls introduced by the London County Council in 1951 during the Festival of Britain are of a splendid pattern, although their shape is perhaps better suited to spring bulbs and harlequin plantings of red, pink, mauve and white ivy-leaf geraniums. Urastone tubs, in all shapes and designs, are cheap and long lasting and can, of course, be painted white for gaiety.

Fibreglass Containers

These are the élite and pick of modern urns and troughs, the products of one company being perfect copies of sixteenth-century and later lead garden ornaments taken from the original moulds. They are strong, frost-proof, light, delightful and expensive. The perfect setting for the reproduction of a lead garden tank is alongside an old pink brick wall with the urn perched above on a becoming pier.

Plastic Containers

Plastics as garden containers abound for those who fancy the material. They have the advantage of retaining the heat, keeping the soil at a more constant temperature than their earthenware counterparts and reducing the toil of watering. They are now to be had in colours brash and kind.

Anyone considering one of these should visit a garden centre or the gardening department of a large store for the choice nowadays of such containers, tubs, troughs, etc., is wide.

Planting in Containers

Late October is an ideal time for planting when the soil is still warm and friable. But plants in the big cities are usually happier if they arrive in the spring. It is important to start off with a good soil mixture and my earlier remarks on soil (see p. 12) should be noted. Crocking should be carried out with care, for it is vital to keep the drainage holes free.

Top-dressing is necessary once or possibly twice a year, scraping away tired soil from the surface and replacing it with a good rich mixture. A rose fertiliser should be given once a week from the time buds form until the flowers open.

If the roses are sprayed with insecticide in early May, as a preventive spray even if the enemy has not yet arrived, the gardener will be saved trouble later on. I have noted that London roses appear to be attacked particularly early in the season.

What to Grow

Strong-growing hybrid teas such as Wendy Cussons, Ena Harkness, Bettina and the stalwart Peace are eminently suitable for this kind of cultivation. The soft pink floribunda Vera Dalton and the dark velvet Red Dandy possess much of the charm of Ena Harkness, are tidy growers and likely to fall in with this type of cultivation.

But for the lead containers something more eighteenth-century might be more in character. I would like to recommend the china rose Cécile Brunner with sprays of miniature flesh-pink flowers of exquisite shape, only growing to 18 inches.

Little White Pet, a perpetual-flowering dwarf, that appeared in 1879 is a gem which would be another good choice. The flowers are creamy-white pompons and the foliage dark and neat: a delightful dwarf in every way. The less seen Cramoisie Picotée, of an even earlier date, has brilliant carmine, full and reflexing flowers with a telling green eye; and growing to a height of about 2 feet, it deserves to be given a chance.

Fragrance

We look to the rose for scent for it is a flower that has always been closely associated with fragrance. It is grossly unfair and uninformed to say that the modern rose has lost its scent. The nurseryman can rightly claim that there are more scented roses listed in his catalogue today than ever before. He can remind those who complain that Frau Karl Druschki and other Victorian highlights cannot hold a sniff to them.

On the other hand, it has to be reluctantly admitted that few modern roses have the strong, heady perfume of the damask roses, but this is not from want of trying. There was, perhaps, a period some fifty years ago when the breeder seemingly lost his head about colour and concentrated on this attribute. The majority of nurserymen are convinced that colour rather than fragrance makes a best seller and will point out that the rose of the century, Peace, has but a moderate to poor scent.

However, fortunately for us the Royal National Rose Society do not favour the scentless rose and seldom award a hybrid tea without any fragrance a trial ground certificate, although on occasion they are lenient towards floribundas. Without this certificate a newcomer is unlikely to make the top grade.

The trouble is that although the hybridizer is as anxious to breed fragrant varieties as those who wish to have them in their garden, he is bedevilled as to how to select the right genes. The information he has to work on is not enlightening for many of the most heavily scented varieties such as Crimson Glory come from but slightly scented forebears.

It is to the breeders credit that he has given the, until recently, unscented floribundas a variety of scents – spicey, fruity, apple or lemon aromas and strange tangs – but although the pundits murmur a host of aldehydes, no one has yet the secret where they come from. When, in 1963, the floribunda Elizabeth of Glamis, a cinnamon scented variety, was awarded the Clay Vase for the sweetest scented new rose of the year, it was indeed a triumph for Sam McGredy.

The further problem in this field is the assessment of scent. Just as tea tasters are trained rather than born, the inner nose membranes which are stationed above the roof of the mouth and between the eye sockets can be educated and tuned to a high sensitivity of sense of smell by use, special training and experience. There is a wide divergence between people's natural gift in detecting subtle odours and there are some unfortunates who cannot distinguish the smell of treasured Rose de Meaux from dead dog. The best way for the amateur to test his powers is to hold a bloom in his warm cupped hands, exhale into the flower and then inhale with his mouth closed.

The Royal National Rose Society awards points for scent to new introductions by taking a majority vote of judges that gives a desirable cross-section of opinion. Unfortunately, the fairness of the system falls down because of the differing stages of the blooms, the half-open flower possessing far more fragrance than the full-opened, so that scent can only be roughly assessed.

The hybrid tea Ena Harkness and the floribundas Red Dandy and Rosemary Rose, arranged by Sheila Macqueen

The cinnamon-scented floribunda Elizabeth of Glamis

Fragrant Cloud, a fine dusky scarlet hybrid tea variety which is noted for its scent

Wendy Cussons, a cerise-red hybrid tea with delightful fragrance and difficult to fault

Summing up, marks must go to the damasks, gallicas, centifolias, musks and albas. Also to the modern red roses, and among them Josephine Bruce, Crimson Glory, Ena Harkness, George Dickson, Wendy Cussons, Madame Louis Laperrière and Fragrant Cloud – as fast as I think of one, another springs to mind.

The best place to smell a rose is in the garden, and anyone still doubtful of the modern rose's fragrance should visit Queen Mary's Rose Garden, Regent's Park, at about 7 a.m. on a damp morning after a night's rain, when the sun has had time to dry the petals. He will soon, I am quite certain, be convinced.

Pot-pourri

Gardeners wishing to make pot-pourri may be glad of a recipe. Roses, preferably of the old-fashioned varieties – the gallicas, damasks and others with a strong scent – should be gathered early in the morning as soon as the sun has dried the petals and before the blooms are fully open. Other flowers picked to go with them should include lavender, with the lower half of the spikes at their zenith; a spray or two of myrtle, rosemary, thyme and sweet briar; a few geranium leaves, and perhaps a leaf or two of mint. These should be spread out on sheets of paper to dry in the sun with the shredded peel of an orange and lemon. When the flowers and leaves are thoroughly dry, mix with 1 lb. kitchen salt and $\frac{1}{2}$ lb. bay-salt, add 1 oz. powdered orris root, half a teaspoonful each of allspice and ground cloves and a pinch of nutmeg.

A layer of this mixture should be placed at the bottom of an earthenware jar and a layer of $\frac{1}{2}$ to 1 inch of the petals added, then a further layer of the salty mixture and a further layer of petals and so on until the jar is full. The mixture should then be covered closely and left for a week or so, stirring it occasionally with a fork. Some gardeners add a few drops of rose essence, 1 oz. of bergamot or perhaps a tablespoonful of eau de cologne or lavender water to the mixture at this stage before packing the pot-pourri into jars, bowls or bags, but these additions are likely to mask the more delicate scents.

Pot-pourri is said to last for years if well made and stoppered, but the essential oils evaporate and the mixture is too often left to become musty as well as dusty.

Part Four

The Old Roses
Species and Their Hybrids
Rose Arrangement
Royal National Rose Society

The Old Roses

The old-timers have stamina, charm and beauty, but fragrance is not a *sine qua non*. To classify these roses in a tidy way is not possible; they overlap, while many varieties remain obscure and untraced. Having been pushed aside for several decades their revival is almost complete and once again they have an honoured place in any distinguished garden.

The common complaint that the old roses flower but once at mid-summer is not wholly fair for the Bourbons bloom more or less continuously through the summer months. Be this as it may, their four weeks' performance compares well with that of any other flowering shrub.

Another grumble is that the old roses are untidy. I would add to this that theirs, if cared for, is a graceful disorder with none of the winter gawkiness of its modern relations. No one can describe the beds of hybrid teas or floribundas in winter a beautiful sight. But comparisons are silly – let us rejoice that the old roses are back again.

Those who wish to know more about the shrub species should visit Murrell's Portland Nurseries, Shrewsbury and Sunningdale Nurseries, Windlesham, Surrey, the leading nurseries that specialise in them. If unable to do this, then their catalogues, with all the fascinating period names, will help to give you a picture of the unsurpassed beauty, so cheaply available.

slight shortening of the laterals that have borne the last season's bloom will suffice.

Maiden's Blush, the endearing Cuisse de Nymphe Emue, now widely grown, is also of the *alba* tribe. Königin Von Dänemark opens from a carmine bud to a heavy quartered pink bloom. It is very double and beautifully fragrant and is one of the great roses. It grows 4 to 5 feet tall.

Madame Legras de St. Germain, with thornless arching stems and neat leaves, has a flat camellia-like white flower with a clear yellow flush in the centre and is one of the elect. This variety reaches a height of 6 to 7 feet.

Königin Von Dänemark which opens from a carmine bud to a heavy quartered pink bloom

The Alba Roses

This group including the white rose of England, *R. alba,* is closely associated with this country. But the origin of *R. alba* is still obscure; it seems likely that it was imported to England from somewhere in the Near East for medicinal purposes because of its powerful scent.

Later on in the Middle Ages, regarded as a native of England, *R. alba semi-plena* was adopted by the House of York as their family emblem. These robust *alba* shrubs, true to type with distinctive grey-green foliage, bear white to pink flowers of great delicacy, oval heps and, in most cases, curved thorns. They need little pruning and a

The Gallicas

Rosa gallica was grown in the temples of the Persians as early as the 12th century B.C. and the 'mad Gallicas' were more grown than any other rose until the nineteenth century and freely cultivated in Provins for medicinal purposes. The deep crimsons and purples are superbly rich, and the pinks, which are rare, have a special delicacy. There are beautiful colour patterns, marbled and striped.

The globular double flowers, small by today's standards, arrive in ones or threes along the canes of the stalwart lateral branches and have a sweet, spicy scent. They are borne on strong foot-stalks

Above: R. gallica versicolor *(Rosa Mundi)—gay, profuse and spectacular*
Below: *The richly-scented Bourbon variety Souvenir de la Malmaison*

The lovely pure white Damask rose Madame Hardy, with lavender and Lilium candidum in the foreground

Top: The plum crimson Gallica variety Charles de Mills
Above: The pale pink Fantin Latour, a Centifolia variety

and the leaves that embrace them are rounded and of a light green. The gallicas are compact and the thorns, when they come, are no more than prickles. This section of roses seldom reaches more than 3 to 4 feet in height. Flowered shoots should be cut back moderately after flowering to encourage young growth from the base.

The gallicas are low-maintenance roses content on the poorest of soils. The dusky-purple Cardinal de Richelieu, very double and showing a white centre when fully open, is one of the best known varieties of this type. As the bloom ages, the dark purple creeps over the flower's face until it becomes velvet-black. Its height is 4 feet. Charles de Mills, velvet plum-crimson, full-petalled and opulent, is another wonder, its height about 3 feet. R. gallica versicolor (Rosa Mundi, often wrongly named York and Lancaster) with flat, brilliantly striped carmine, pale pink or white flowers is gay profuse and spectacular. Height about 3 to 4 feet.

Rosa gallica officinalis, the Apothecary's Rose and the Red Rose of Lancaster, is a rewarding shrub, dating from the Roman Empire: upright, and bushy; the semi-double light-crimson flowers

are decorated with yellow stamens. The heps that follow are showy. It makes a bush some 4 feet high and as much across. The date of introduction of Tuscany is unknown. It is the dark maroon 4-foot-tall 'Old Velvet' rose and the darkest of a deep-coloured group. Erect and neat it is a startling rose and a treasure.

The Gallicas will survive so long as there are rosarians around to grow them.

The Damasks

The Damask roses, which came almost certainly from the Gallicas, were spoken of by the Greeks, Herodotus and Theophrastus, and were continuously grown through the ages. Their popularity was undoubtedly due to their dominant attar-of-rose scent. They are said to have been brought to Europe from Damascus by the Crusaders.

The foliage is greyer than that of the Gallicas and more lax, the flowers pink to white, semi-double and double, and their fragrance is that of the best of our roses to-day. It could be said that the modern rose derived its scent from the damasks.

The exquisite, fragrant Moss Rose, R. centifolia muscosa, *showing the 'moss' on the calyx and stems*

The flowers of this group are short-stalked and sit comfortably on downy rounded leaves; the heps that follow are long and narrow.

Madame Hardy is my pick of the Damasks. The flowers, of purest white, are borne in clusters and are very double. Their attractions are enhanced by their small green eyes, and they have a fresh lemon scent. This variety flowers profusely in early summer and it makes a bush 5 to 6 feet tall. Quatre Saisons is said to have been grown at Pompeii and is the famous one-and-only autumn-flowering Damask. The soft pink flowers have little quality but are beautifully scented and it is a rose rarely caught out of bloom. Its height is 4 feet. York and Lancaster, sometimes pink, sometimes bluish-white, is a rose with a great history that should only be attempted by the rosarian on good strong soil. Otherwise it is likely to be a poor flowerer sans stripes.

The Centifolias

These are the Cabbage roses, madly popular with gardeners for centuries, and it has been said that they were grown in Holborn as far back as 1596.

The group originated in Holland just when the great school of Dutch painters dedicated themselves to still-life and floral pictures. The Centifolias, globular, nodding with dignity on graceful curved stems became their Queen, and the Painter's Rose.

Rosa centifolia, The Rose of a Hundred Leaves, seen in many paintings of the Old Masters has large, lax leaves, coarsely toothed. The smooth, pink, drooping, deep-centred flowers are bursting with petals and scent, the stems weakened by their weight. Obviously a flower so made may disappoint in a wet summer. It grows to 5 feet tall. Chapeau de Napoléon, with the edges of its sepals crested, is a lovely rose-pink, graceful and fragrant period rose. Fantin Latour is a very double pale pink variety, opening flat with infolded centres while Unique Blanche or White Provence, a true Centifolia type, is free-flowering and the best white. Chapeau de Napoléon and Fantin Latour reach a height of 6 feet, and Unique Chapeau, 4 to 5 feet.

The Moss Roses

Rosa centifolia muscosa, the Moss Rose, is a fascinating sport of the Cabbage Rose that appeared in the eighteenth century. The deep silky 'moss' on calyx and stems varies in colour from rich green to dark red. The interest shown in the Moss Roses in the nineteenth century led to the raising of hundreds of hybrids which are mainly June to July flowering and with a rich, fruity scent. Many of the pink varieties are irresistible, the long encrusted buds opening into globular blooms to show a button eye. Some of the modern hybrids, although providing a wider range of colour, lack the veteran's charm.

Old Pink Moss, a 5 to 6-foot-tall rose with heavy scent, was a smash hit in 1727 – and little wonder. It is exquisite. The variety Blanche Moreau, in which the buds are covered with dark red 'moss,' gives an occasional autumn flower if well tended. It grows to a height of 6 feet. Little Gem is a light crimson miniature that makes a pleasant small bush of 2 to 3 feet, and Nuits de Young, with maroon-purple, double flowers of velvet quality, is one of the famous mosses lit up by a ring of yellow stamens. Its height is 3 to 4 feet.

Species & Their Hybrids

These are the wild roses and primogenitors of the modern rose. Many of them come from Himalayan Asia and all possess great stamina that has brought them through the ages.

Remarkably disease free the species are easy to please and content with any reasonably fertile soil provided they get air and light and plenty of sunshine. They ask for little attention – an annual dressing of manure plus a sprinkling of a balanced fertiliser, and light pruning, only dead and exhausted wood being removed.

Informal in habit, the wild roses are happy among other shrubs and, without prejudice, they will usually be found more accommodating than their neighbours. Perhaps they look their best in the wild garden or in a wasted corner with a sympathetic setting where they can be left to go their own way.

The species, usually single-flowered, have a simplicity and beauty all their own, far removed from the stylised and elegant twentieth century rose: they are in no way interchangeable or comparable. It is a group of roses of rich variety that will grow from 3 to 12 feet, scramble its way through the trees or just hug the earth.

There are as many as 220 species left to us. The status of species, sub-species and hybrids are difficult to determine but I have recently been comforted by a specialist on old roses who told me perfect nomenclature was no longer possible.

Once you take the Old Roses to your heart, a specialist nursery should be visited in June or July so that you can make your own choice as a fair description of their colour, shape and texture defeats most of us who write about them. In certain parts of Britain, *R. canina* the native single dog rose, may be seen waving its light pink flowers in the hedgerows. Viewed against a blue sky it is superb, as sweet both to the nose as the eye. *R. moyesii,* when satisfied with its surroundings, can be equally profuse and carefree, and its dusky red flowers and bottle-shaped heps are telling and decorative. But if for some reason this rose is frustrated I should warn that it becomes gaunt and unbending. In any case, patience is needed for *moyesii* is slow to settle down.

The lacy foliage and bottle-shaped heps of R. moyesii, *a rose which is profuse and carefree when satisfied*

Below: *The heps of* R. moyesii *in close-up*
Bottom: *The dusky red flowers of* R. moyesii

Rosa ecae from Afghanistan possesses one of the most brilliant yellows found among roses. Its minute leaves make a delicate background for the buttercup-like spring flowers, and the prominent red thorns make the plant easily distinguishable. It is a very erect, slender rose, 5 feet tall, that provides an arresting display in May.

Those looking for scent and simplicity should go in search of *R. macrantha* Lady Curzon, a single pink variety that will grow into a 7 to 8-foot bush and flood the air with its delicious fragrance in June.

I have already said something about the glories of climbing *R. filipes* and its giant form Kiftsgate; the ground-hugging *R. paulii* (which can also be grown on posts), with its starry white flowers; the gaiety of hedgemaker Canary Bird; and the modern hybrid spinossissimas that Wilhelm Kordes and other hybridists have sent us from Germany. I close, for fun, with two extra-ordinaries from China – *R. chinensis mutabilis* and *R. viridiflora*.

Rosa chinensis mutabilis (Tipo Idéale) is a chameleon of muted pastel shades, with yellow-orange buds that pass through soft yellow to sunset-pink. In fact it is a distinguished and aesthetic Masquerade that fits in more amicably with neighbours than the modern counterpart of the Circus fraternity. Where this rose originated we do not know, but it is a wild rose of 8 feet in height with immense charm that should be given a place wherever it will grow.

Lastly *R. viridiflora*, the Green Rose, a curious China rose whose origin has not been altogether satisfactorily established. Its flowers are whorls of sepals and there are no petals at all. It is, therefore, seen at its best at the budding stage before its quasi-petals turn to red-brown. Completely sterile, *viridiflora* is a botanical curiosity and by no means beautiful – just a funny ha-ha!.

The Bourbons

The Bourbons were the happy result of a chance cross between the China and Damask roses during the eighteenth century. It was this cross that led to the first perpetual-flowering roses that fortunately maintained their damask scent and distinction.

Since this group is perpetual-flowering, February pruning is advised.

Some gardeners may feel that the Bourbons have been out-classed by the Hybrid Perpetuals and Hybrid Teas that they helped to bring into being. But the handful that remain to us are of such perfection that they are likely to stay in our gardens for all time.

I have a particular affection for the 5 foot tall Boule de Neige as it was the first rose I ever grew. The full ivory-white camellia-shaped flowers are exquisite and perpetual. Commandant Beaurepaire, about a foot taller, is a brilliant deep pink with red and purple stripes. It is a sweetly exciting variety that gives a second but thinner performance in the autumn. Mme Pierre Oger, also 6 feet tall, varies from rose-pink to deep rose in colour, according to the weather conditions. It is a shell-like flower with a lovely scent.

Large, flat and very fully quartered, Souvenir de la Malmaison, with blush coloured flowers deepening to flesh-pink in the centre, makes a sensational pillar rose. It flowers continuously and is richly scented. Its height as a bush is 3 to 4 feet. And the best-loved Bourbon of all is the rosy-cerise, thornless Zéphirine Drouhin, with rare fragrance, that will surely be with us forever.

Austrian Briars

This group have already been mentioned earlier (see p. 104) but something must be said about *Rosa lutea* (syn. *R. foetida*), so well represented by the two-toned flame-orange Austrian Copper and Austrian Yellow.

Although the blooms are small the effect of their spring bloom is glorious and the yellow form is hard to beat for colour. But the 'Austrians' are only at their best in a warm garden in a mild district. They reach about 6 feet in height.

The Musk Roses

The musk roses have also been mentioned in the section on hedges (p. 105) but this is an opportunity to add two more of my favourite musks to the lists, both particularly valuable because of their robustness. The white-flowered Prosperity whose petals are tinged with gold and the deep pink Vanity are a magnificent sight in bloom when fully grown. Both reach a height of 6 to 7 feet.

The starry white flowers of R. paulii, *a ground-hugging variety which can also be trained on supports. This very thorny rose provides dense cover*

The Sweet Briars

Rosa rubiginosa is primarily a hedge-making shrub, but La Belle Distinguée with its double bright crimson flowers is a beauty although not so vigorous as the Penzance varieties. Its height is 3 to 4 feet.

The Scots Briars

Here, *R. spinosissima*, with double, blush-pink flowers 2 to 3 inches across and wonderfully scented, deserves special mention. It is perpetual-flowering but is unfortunately rather a sparse grower. The height reached is 4 feet.

Modern Shrub Roses

Finally, a small rag bag of cross-bred roses that no longer seem to fit in with the moderns. They are all very desirable and I would not like my book or garden to be without them:

BONN: coral-scarlet, a perpetual flowerer and a vivid bush when in bloom. Height, 4 to 5 feet.

CONSTANCE SPRY: a pink Centifolia type of tremendous harm. A superb rose with every virtue. Height, 6 to 7 feet.

DORTMUND: a Kordes perpetual-flowering rose. A single red with a white eye blooming in great profusion. Height, 5 to 6 feet.

JOSEPH'S COAT: a semi-climber with double golden yellow flowers flushed with orange and the petals edged with red. This rose gives a generous second performance in the autumn and has the advantage of being disease resistant.

The Bourbon rose Madame Pierre Oger

Constance Spry, a pink Centifolia type rose of great charm and with every virtue

Joseph's Coat

MARGUERITE HILLING: a pink sport of Nevada. Height 6 to 7 feet.

NEVADA: A beautiful rose with *R. moyesii* as one of its parents; cream opening to white with splendid golden stamens. A wonderful sight when in flower and an acquisition for any garden. Height, 6 to 7 feet.

NYMPHENBURG: a salmon-pink perpetual-flowerer tinted gold. This is an attractive, vigorous shrub. Height 6 to 7 feet.

In any such list as this there will be personal likes and dislikes, but in my opinion these seven moderns all possess rose-magic.

MUSIC TO THE EAR

The prettiest compliment ever paid by man to woman: 'Won't you come into the garden? I would like my roses to see you.' Sheridan.

Right: *Delphiniums, phlox, scabious, marjoram and other border plants in perfect harmony with soft-coloured roses*

Arrangements by Sheila Macqueen
Below: *An arrangement of the varieties Helen Traubel, Beauté, Sir Lancelot and Glory of Ceylon*

Below: *Ballota, jasmine, variegated honeysuckle and other plants make an elegant frame for the burnt-orange Fantan, Beauté and Sutter's Gold*

Rose Arrangement

The most important of all summer flowers are the roses. It is not necessary for me to press their beauty, but I ask flower arrangers to do them justice. We seem to be suffering an unfortunate patch just now in floral decoration, and in the reckless search for originality, flower arrangement has become disastrously gimmicky.

As Connie Spry often pointed out, roses look their best when allowed to speak for themselves. Her own cascades of roses were irresistible, her vegetable bowls of Caroline Testout with two or three black-red velvet species at the heart of the bunch were ravishing while escaping the chocolate-box look; her handling of delicate white roses, usually kept apart from pinks or reds, will be remembered by all who saw them.

Connie Spry was a knowledgeable horticulturist and a flower reformer to whom we can never be sufficiently grateful. She gave gardeners new eyes and set the flowers free from the stiff decor of the nineteenth century – the imprisoned carnations, Maidenhair and *Asparagus plumosus* (Asparagus Fern), the narrow necked silver epergne and the small tables bespattered with photographs with sweet peas and gypsophilia peeping round the silver frames. She swept the narrow-necked vases back into the cupboard and taught us to make use of exciting containers, encouraged her followers to employ ordinary garden or even wild flowers, and fruit and foliage which had never been seen in the drawing-room before. The vegetables, the variegated kales and silver-headed onions, artichoke and wild carrot came into their own.

Bells and silver foliage were used at Christmas time but accessories were incidental, the general ruling being that the material should be flowers, fruit and foliage. The flood gate opened, flower arrangement became first the fashion, then the rage.

Alas, when Connie Spry went, although her influence stayed, it faded and her restraint and sensitive taste were sadly missed. Exacting rules, technical mumbo-jumbo and a great deal of talk about a 'focal point' crept in, and the decline in the art was quickened by competitions staged by floral societies when the arrangement entered had to conform and be related to such titles as 'Mainly for Women,' 'The Cruel Sea,' Situations Vacant,' 'The Promising Future,' 'Sports Page' and so on.

It distresses many flower lovers to see a floral exhibit entered as 'Dad's Retirement' – presenting pipe, pouch, matches, bottle, glass and cork with a few chrysanthemums tucked in here and there. And a few yards away in another niche, a cushion of mixed asters under the heading 'Dad's Good-bye.' This sort of thing sans taste and humour has lowered the standing of flower arrangement and brought it into disrepute.

I have a memory of a man looking bedevilled at a hideous interpretation entitled 'Hell.' It was of red-hot-pokers and thistles along with a whip, chains and flick-knives – 'Another Constance Spry' the onlooker sadly sighed, little knowing that Connie would have been more shocked by the wretched decoration than he was.

Summing up, I now risk putting a personal opinion, by suggesting that the time has come for a clear and strict division between floral art and what might be known as 'florage.' (In the same way that paintings that include accessories such as wire netting, studs and nails are aptly described as 'collage').

Floral art should surely remain an art dealing with flowers, fruit and foliage.

'Florage' that gives so much pleasure to so many, stimulating the imagination of the semi- and even the non-flower arranger, should go forward under the new title, introducing anything from a goldfish to a greenfly, drapes, bagpipes, boots, bottles – the pleasing and unpleasing. But such an ensemble should be kept apart from serious floral arrangement, and not allowed to destroy the image of the serious arranger and make a fool of him.

There is no need to urge the decorative value of the old-fashioned rose and the species; they know what they want to do and often arrange themselves. The moderns are less co-operative. Of the twentieth-century whites, I put the floribunda Ice-

Right: *A decorative wreath of* R. gallica complicata, *a pink variety with golden stamens, arranged by Marny Macintosh*

Below: *A dish arrangement by Marny Macintosh of the rich yellow, spring-flowering shrub rose, Canary Bird*

berg first. But Message is a lovely hybrid tea with an enchanting green translucence and Virgo is rewarding in a fine summer. Pascali is an easy doer but is flesh-tinted rather than white. Among yellow roses, the floribunda Allgold is forever in bloom, and Spek's Yellow with its greenish bud and unique golden-yellow flower will be found very telling in the most exalted company.

Flower decorators who prefer pastel shades are faithful to Paul's Lemon Pillar: those who find Peace a trifle opulent will prefer Grand'mère Jenny. Meanwhile, the deep yellow Summer Sunshine is a favourite with flower arrangers and abundant in bloom.

Queen Elizabeth must surely head the list of the pinks, with the floribunda Dearest as a second best and double Rosemary Rose, a large, double, pink-cerise with red foliage, an attractive third. Popular Perfecta, an ivory shaded pink hybrid tea, can be a wonder, usually improving towards the end of the season, but unfortunately it cannot be relied upon.

Margaret has line and distinction, Madame Butterfly and her Lady Sylvia progeny have an air of romance; Wendy Cussons is a striking and splendid hard pink with a damask scent, but its colour makes it a dangerous companion.

Little Cécile Brunner is a darling and ideal for small and miniature vases. Ena Harkness, Ernest H. Morse, Madame Louis Laperrière and Josephine Bruce are all heavenly, and for those who wish for a startling and intense vermilion there is Super Star.

Among the orange-shaded there is the desirable apricot-orange Mojave; Bettina, a flaming rose with a golden base; and Zambra a true orange, but vulnerable to mildew. My pick of this group is Beauté, orange-flushed yellow with shapely buds and graceful flowers. Lastly, Fantan, an unusual burnt-orange, a new shade that has been warmly welcomed.

Polychromes and bi-colours there are in plenty for those looking for the bizarre. Piccadilly, bright scarlet and gold, must be the number one bicolour; and perhaps scarlet and gold Tzigane the runner up.

The lilac roses that some raisers descend to calling blue include Africa Star, Blue Moon, Sterling Silver, Lavender, Pinocchio and single and beautiful Lilac Charm with golden anthers. Cut in bud, the single flowers hold quite well. Grey Pearl, a lavender-grey, shaded olive green and tan, well shaped and reflexing, captivates or repels.

I cannot close without a word of gratitude to the Garnette roses, beloved by the florist and the best-lasting roses we have. I have known red Garnette and its pink counterpart Carol last fresh in a vase for over a fortnight. The flowers' shape and the stiff flower petals may, alas, lack glamour, but a bunch from time to time when the budget is tight is a sound and helpful buy.

Should heps be wanted for decoration, the bottle-shaped fruits of *R. moyesii* are my first choice.

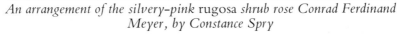

An arrangement of the silvery-pink rugosa *shrub rose Conrad Ferdinand Meyer, by Constance Spry*

Above: *The floribunda rose Iceberg in an arrangement by Ann Ord*

Above: *The floribunda variety Plentiful, arranged by the author*

Below: *The hybrid tea variety Fragrant Cloud, arranged with cryptanthus and* Begonia rex, *by Sheila Macqueen*

Royal National Rose Society

The first Grand National Rose Show was held at St. James' Piccadilly on the present site of the Piccadilly Hotel in 1858 and was attended by over 2,000 visitors. From then onwards, annual shows – some more successful than others, took place and the Society, formed in 1876, prospered until the outbreak of the First World War when membership fell dramatically. However, Courtney Page, the Secretary, nursed the Society back to health and in 1929 over 250 new varieties bloomed at the Society's first Trial Ground.

In the summer of 1955, a total membership of 45,000 was announced and the National Rose Society now became the largest and most important specialists' horticultural society in the world, with H.R.H. The Princess Royal as its Patron. The membership at the time of writing is over 116,000.

The objects of the Society are to spread the knowledge of the rose and rose growing and to improve and extend its cultivation by scientific trials; to hold exhibitions and issue publications. In addition to the publications, there are free tickets to members for the Great Summer and Autumn Show and a large number of the affiliated societies throughout the country, while books may be borrowed from a well-stocked library and advice from competent experts is given.

But to my mind, the most important function and service of the Society (now the Royal National Rose Society) is the testing and evaluation of new varieties prior to their introduction into commerce.

Raisers send their new varieties, six of each variety, to St. Albans, from all over the world. The plants stay for three years and certificates may be granted in the second or third year. No awards are made in the first year, but records of the plant's behaviour and habits are carefully kept. At the end of the third year, the plants are lifted and burnt, the soil treated and rested before a new supply of varieties are introduced.

The Test Ground at St. Albans is open and exposed to the north, east and south but there is some slight wind-break to the west.

Any variety receiving an award can be considered suitable for garden purposes in most districts of the British Isles. This is invaluable information for the amateur who has been so often led up the garden path by enthusiastic salesmen.

The modest annual subscription is a magnificent investment.

A table arrangement of roses

Part of the Royal National Rose Society's garden and its headquarters at Chiswell Green Lane, St. Albans, Hertfordshire

A view of the Rose Garden at Luton Hoo, Luton, Bedfordshire

Rose Terms and Definitions

BEDDING ROSE: varieties of fairly bushy uniform growth suitable for formal bedding.

BORDER: often applied to the larger specimen roses that look well in the border but would swamp a bed and give an uneven performance.

BUD: this may either be a flower or a leaf bud containing the embryo flower or leaf.

EYE: the rosarian's term for an undeveloped leaf bud.

BUDDING: a method of grafting used to create a garden rose by uniting a bud of the variety with the root system of a strong-growing rose. The budding scion consists of one bud only attached to a small portion of bark. The prepared bud of the desired variety is inserted under the bark of a rootstock and bound in position with soft raffia or twine.

DOUBLE BLOOMS: blooms possessing 18 to 30 petals.

FULL-PETALLED: a rose possessing 30-45 petals.

HEELING-IN: planting temporarily until permanent planting can be undertaken should the roses arrive during unfavourable weather or the beds be unready to receive them. If the roots are carefully covered with soil the roses will come to no harm for several weeks.

LATERAL: a side shoot or branch in contrast to a main or leading terminal shoot.

LEADER: the shoot that terminates a branch.

MAIDEN: a tree in its first year. Maiden growth is the tree's first year's growth.

OVARY: the seed vessel.

REVERSION: a term used by gardeners when a sport that has been highly developed by selection reverts to an earlier form (a throwback in colour to either of its parents).

ROOTSTOCKS: selected rose species that have proved themselves adequate for budding purposes.

SCION: the leaf buds (eyes) of the cultivated variety used for budding, or any bud separated from its parent and grafted to another plant.

SEEDLING: a rose raised from seed.

SEMI-DOUBLE: blooms possessing more than five but not more than 18 petals.

SINGLE-FLOWERED: a bloom possessing one row of five petals.

SNAG: an unwanted stump, often the result of unsatisfactory pruning.

SPORT: a freak of nature or any variation from the normal, usually a flower making a sudden appearance on a stem differing in colour from that of its parent.

SPORT CLIMBER: a sport that appears unheralded with climbing characteristics on a rose bush.

STANDARDS: hybrid teas or floribundas budded on selected stems several feet high. Full standards are budded on 3 ft. 6 in. stems; half-standards on about 2 ft. stems, and dwarfs on stems measuring less than this.

SUCKERS: growths coming from the understock or rootstock.

SUMMER FLOWERING: usually denotes those varieties that flower but once during the season.

STAMEN: the stamen is the male organ of the flower made up of a thin stalk and a head known as the anther. It is the anther which is the pollen bearing organ.

STIGMA: the end of the pistil or female organ on which the pollen is retained.

STYLE: the stem of the pistil that joins the stigma to the ovary.

UNION: the point where the bud and rootstock are joined together.

WEEPING STANDARDS: rambler roses budded on about 5-foot stems from which the top growth is trained to hang down or weep so that they would appear to be of a pendulous habit.

Acknowledgements

I am especially grateful to Mrs Sheila Macqueen for her beautiful arrangements reproduced in this book, and to Mr John Miller of *Country Life,* for his photographs of them. I am also much indebted to my friends Mr E. B. LeGrice, Mr S. M. Gault, M.B.E., F.L.S., V.M.H., Miss H. Murrell and Mr L. Turner for their advice and kindness in reading the manuscript, and, of course, to my secretary, Dorothy Hobden.

My thanks go to Mrs Marny Macintosh and Miss Ann Ord and to all the photographers and organisations who have loaned or given permission for photographs to be used, namely:

Mr B. Alfieri
BLACK AND WHITE: p42 top.

Amateur Gardening
COLOUR: p62; BLACK AND WHITE: p16 top and centre, p17 bottom, p18 bottom right, p20, p21, p22, p23, p24, p26, p27, p28, p29, p34, p37, p38, p39, p40, p41, p42 bottom, p43, p47, pp48 and 49, p52, p54, p58 centre, p60 bottom, p69, p71 bottom, p72, p73, p76 top, p77 bottom right, p80, p83 top right, p86 right, p88 top, p93 top, p97, p101 bottom, p102, p106 top, p108, p110 left, p111 left, p116, p120 top right, p122 top and bottom right and p125 top right.

Mr H. M. Carter
COLOUR: p107 top.

W. H. Collins, Sons and Co. Ltd.
BLACK AND WHITE: p99 top right.

Mr R. J. Corbin
BLACK AND WHITE: p25 and p92 left.

Daily Mirror
COLOUR: p67 bottom, p83 top left, p91 and p99 top left; BLACK AND WHITE: pp48 and 49 and p76 bottom right.

J. M. Dent and Sons Ltd.
BLACK AND WHITE: p130 (from Constance Spry's *Flowers in House and Garden*)

Mr J. E. Downward
COLOUR: p15 bottom and p107 bottom; BLACK AND WHITE: p13, p17 top, p58 bottom left, p60 top left, p61 top right and centre bottom, p65 right, p77 top right, p82, p83 bottom, p89 top, p93 bottom, p98 bottom, p104 top right, p125 top and bottom left and p133.

Mary Evans Picture Library
ETCHING: p11, p103 and p117.

The Field
BLACK AND WHITE: p19, p78 and 79, p85, p87, p120 left and p124.

C. Gregory and Son Ltd.
COLOUR: p59 bottom, p90 bottom left, p90 and p91.

R. Harkness and Son Ltd.
BLACK AND WHITE: p86 left.

Mr A. J. Huxley
BLACK AND WHITE: p88 bottom, p92 right, p106 bottom and p118.

E. B. LeGrice Ltd.
COLOUR: p74 bottom.

The London News Agency
BLACK AND WHITE: p98 top and p101 top.

Mr R. Malby
BLACK AND WHITE: p18 bottom left.

The Mansell Collection
endpaper illustrations.

S. McGredy and Son Ltd.
BLACK AND WHITE: p114.

Practical Gardening
COLOUR: p15 top.

The Radio Times Hulton Picture Library
BLACK AND WHITE: p66 and p67; ETCHING: p57 and p135.

The Royal National Rose Society
BLACK AND WHITE: p109 right, p110 right and p132.

Mr Harry Smith
COLOUR: frontispiece, p14, pp30 and 31, p59 top, p70, p71 top, p74 top, p78, p90 top left; BLACK AND WHITE: p58 top, p64 top, p65 top left, p76 bottom left, p77 bottom left, p81, p84, p89 bottom, p104 top and bottom left, p105, p109 left, p111 right and p120 bottom right.

Mr G. S. Thomas
BLACK AND WHITE: p104 bottom right.

Mr D. Tilley
BLACK AND WHITE: p122 left.

Universal Rose Selection
BLACK AND WHITE: p58 bottom right and p64 bottom.

Index

Abbreviation: p = photograph